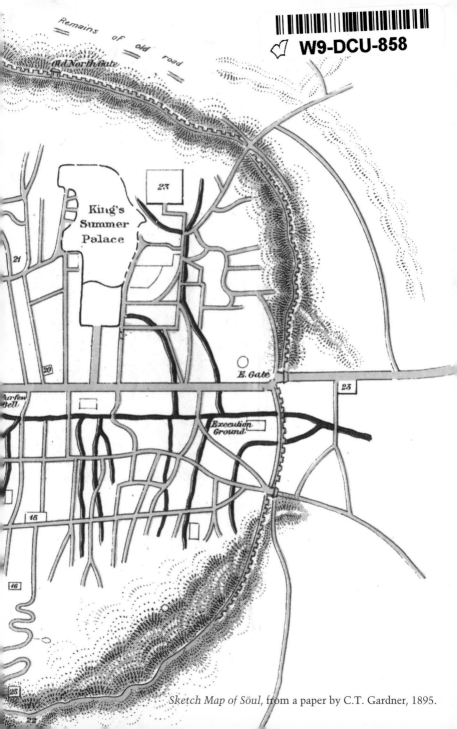

Remains of old road

Old North Gate

23

King's
Summer
Palace

21

20

E. Gate

23

Cur-few
Bell

Execution
Ground

15

16

25

22

Sketch Map of Söul, from a paper by C.T. Gardner, 1895.

St. Olaf College Libraries

IMAGES OF ASIA

Old Seoul

Series Editors, China Titles:
NIGEL CAMERON, SYLVIA FRASER-LU

Old Seoul

KEITH PRATT

OXFORD
UNIVERSITY PRESS

OXFORD
UNIVERSITY PRESS

Oxford University Press is a department of the University of Oxford.
It furthers the University's objective of excellence in research, scholarship,
and education by publishing worldwide in

Oxford New York

Auckland Bangkok Buenos Aires Cape Town Chennai
Dar es Salaam Delhi Hong Kong Istanbul Karachi Kolkata
Kuala Lumpur Madrid Melbourne Mexico City Mumbai Nairobi
São Paulo Shanghai Singapore Taipei Tokyo Toronto

and an associated company in Berlin

Oxford is a registered trade mark of Oxford University Press

Published in the United States
by Oxford University Press Inc., New York

© Oxford University Press 2002

First published 2002
This impression (lowest digit)
1 3 5 7 9 10 8 6 4 2

British Library Cataloguing in Publication Data
available

Library of Congress Cataloging-in-Publication Data
available

ISBN 019-593087-8

Printed in Hong Kong
Published by Oxford University Press (China) Ltd
18th Floor, Warwick House East, Taikoo Place, 979 King's Road, Quarry Bay
Hong Kong

Contents

Acknowledgements

I am grateful to the following owners and publishers who have generously allowed me to reproduce pictures to which they have rights:

Anonymous owner, Plate 1.
British Library, by courtesy of the Trustees, Plates 6 & 23.
Kokusho Kanko-kai, 'Mede Miru Richo-jidai', Figures 1.1, 3.1, 3.8, & 3.10.
Korean Overseas Information Service, Plates 5 & 21.
Lee Doo-Won, Plate 8.
The Moffett Korea Collection, Figures 1.2, 3.3, 3.7, & 3.11.
National Centre for the Performing Arts, Seoul, Plate 24.
The National Museum of Denmark, Ethnographic Collection, Plates 9, 10, &14.
The Royal Geographic Society Archives, Figure 5.3.
Seoul National University Museum, Plate 12.
Hubert D. Vos, Plate 4.
Yonsei University Library, Figures 3.2, 3.4, & 4.1.
Plates 7, 11, 13, 16–22 are from the author's collection.

In some cases it has not been possible, despite every effort, to locate those with rights to material possibly still in copyright. The publisher and author would be glad to hear of anyone who holds such rights, in order that appropriate acknowledgement can be made in any future editions.

A Note on Romanization

For many years, Western books on Korea employed the McCune–Reischauer (MR) system of romanization when transliterating Korean names and words. In 2000, the South Korean government officially adopted a new system. Though this has yet to establish itself in widespread use outside Korea, it is now to be encountered in books and periodicals published there, and on maps and street signs. It is used in this book to assist recognition by readers visiting Korea who may be unfamiliar with MR. MR equivalents are given in the Index at the back of the book.

For Chinese names and terms, the pinyin system of romanization is used.

For Rachel and Timothy

Introduction:
The Joseon Dynasty (1392–1910)

THROUGHOUT THE FIRST millennium AD, Chinese armies, envoys, merchants, and craftsmen spread their country's reputation far and wide. They ensured that across East and South-East Asia Chinese styles and standards were recognized and admired in everything from political systems to town planning, architecture to coinage, written script to painting. Such was the power and fascination of the Middle Kingdom that foreigners were drawn to it. They came to pledge their rulers' recognition to the emperor and his court; to study the Classics of Confucianism in the Imperial Academy and the scriptures of Buddhism on the holy mountains; to trade and settle. Sometimes they even came presumptuously as invaders.

Korea, as one of China's closest neighbours, could not remain immune to its dominating influence. Korean kings acknowledged China by sending tribute gifts and flowery letters couched in subservient terms; Korean scholars studied the Chinese Classics; calligraphers and artists imitated Chinese styles and produced works of art that their Chinese colleagues would have been proud of. Nevertheless, when three non-Chinese dynasties dominated Manchuria and northern China from the tenth to fourteenth centuries, Korea became more pragmatic and loosened its diplomatic ties with China. The leaders of Korea's Goryeo dynasty (918–1392) followed more independent paths than their predecessors, but when the Mongols overwhelmed Korean military resistance (1232–5), completed their conquest of China in 1279, and forced Koreans to help them mount an invasion of Japan, the traditional order in East Asia seemed to be lost forever.

The Mongols' success, however, proved to be short-lived. In 1368 the Chinese threw them out, established the Ming dynasty, and reasserted their regional superiority. Their new leader, the Hongwu Emperor (r.1368–98), was an erstwhile Buddhist monk and rebel leader who quickly consolidated his autocratic régime by grounding it in a rigidly interpreted version of Confucianism. These momentous events inevitably had repercussions in Korea, where the Goryeo rulers, widely condemned for their subservience to the invaders, were toppled by one of their own military officers, Yi Seonggye (1335–1408), who was named king in 1392. He took the title Taejo ('Great Progenitor'), sent tribute to the Ming capital in acknowledgement of the supremacy of the new Chinese dynasty over the Mongols, and asked the Emperor to approve the name of his own new dynasty, Joseon ('Dynastic freshness'). Hongwu was happy to oblige. Symbolic of a fresh start, as well as a return to a site with (pre-Goryeo) historic connections, Taejo moved his capital south-east from Gaeseong to Seoul and began to build a new city there that would become the hub of the nation and, centuries later, one of the world's greatest cities. The dynasty that he had founded would prove to be the most enduring in Korea's history.

Many Koreans felt a sense of relief that the proper world order had been restored after a lapse of several centuries. Buddhism and shamanism had enjoyed considerable influence among the Goryeo rulers, but now the literati welcomed Taejo's nomination of Confucianism as the official orthodoxy for their state, even though the current version, developed in China by Zhu Xi (1130–1200), was laden with unfamiliar rules and regulations. Indeed, so greatly did the early Joseon monarchs exalt neo-Confucianism, as it is known today, that they banned physical evidence of

Buddhism from the new capital city, even refusing entry to monks. Traditional social hierarchies, incorporating male superiority and the pre-eminence of the literati, were reinforced by the revival of Confucian priorities, and the authority of the ruling Yi clan benefited from the early Ming emperors' restoration of regional stability. Perhaps there was no greater exemplar in Korean history of the ideal Confucian king, governing his people wisely and with sympathy, than King Sejong (r. 1418–50). He took a personal interest in agriculture, meteorology, astronomy, and the arts, and among the many achievements credited to him was the invention of the Korean alphabet, *hangeul*, first published in 1444. Inevitably, perhaps, his successors failed to match his example, and under weaker kings the court became torn by political factionalism.

By the late sixteenth century the militant Japanese *daimyo* Toyotomi Hideyoshi, dreaming of ascending the dragon throne in Beijing as the Son of Heaven, saw an increasingly restive Korea as easy prey and a gateway to the continent. In 1592, he invaded. Chinese armies came to Korea's assistance and he was repelled. He tried again in 1597 and the threat to Korea was only lifted when he died in 1598. But the destruction already caused by the wars, in Seoul and across the Korean peninsula, was immense. Korean confidence was badly shaken, all the more so when the Manchus further devastated northern Korea in 1627 and 1636, and then went on to overthrow the Ming and set up the Qing dynasty in China. In Korea the Joseon dynasty survived, but now even some of the literati began to ask hard questions about the value of clinging forever to China's coat-tails. They learned from Jesuit missionaries in China that the outer world offered new intellectual and scientific ideas, and some of them quietly began to explore Catholicism. What these 'radicals' of the so-called *silhak* ('true learning') movement wanted was the right to choose what was best for Korea, whether it came from China or elsewhere. Kings needed to be firm and shrewd if they were to control such liberal scholars as well as ambitious old-style ministers loyal to China and the political factions associated with rival clans. Throughout the eighteenth century, when Korea enjoyed peace and stability, King Yeongjo (r.1724–76) and his grandson Jeongjo (r. 1776–1800) were well in command. Thereafter it was a different story.

By the early nineteenth century the influence of Manchu China had waned and Korean leaders had grown used to taking their own decisions. One of those who preferred to keep things this way was Prince Yi Haeung (1820–98), who plotted to have his son nominated as heir apparent to King Cheoljong. When the boy succeeded to the throne as King Gojong in 1864 at the age of eleven, his father acquired the princely title **Daeweon-gun**[*] and ruled as *de facto* regent until 1873, gaining some popularity for taking measures to curb the powers and privileges of the literati. In 1866 he married his son to an impoverished kinswoman of his wife, a 14-year old girl who thus became Queen Min. But rather than strengthening the Daeweon-gun's own position, as he expected the match to do, it proved to be a miscalculation with tragic consequences. If Gojong himself developed little taste for the rapidly changing and confusing political pattern of the late nineteenth century, his Queen entered into it with gusto, becoming an ardent opponent of her father-in-law (Plates 1 & 2).

---

[*] Words and phrases in bold indicate the first occurrence in the text of a term included in the Glossary.

China, Japan, and Korea all had to confront crises arising from the arrival of Westerners in the nineteenth century. The Daeweon-gun, conscious of their destabilizing effect on even his more powerful neighbours, initially opted for isolationism. But missionary enterprise had already taken root, and in 1866 he ordered a persecution of Catholics. Those martyred in Seoul included the French Bishop Siméon-François Berneux as well as many Koreans. A punitive squadron of French naval vessels, sent from their China station, landed troops on Ganghwa Island at the mouth of the Han River, but they were driven away by Korean soldiers. In the same year, an American merchant steamship ran aground near Pyeongyang and all aboard were killed by local people. A revenge expedition was dispatched from Yokohama in 1871 and was also repulsed, though with heavy Korean losses. Round one had gone to isolationism.

In 1875, however, a more determined Japanese naval attack led to a treaty which significantly breached Korean diplomatic defences. The Treaty of Ganghwa 'freed' Korea, so the Japanese claimed, from traditional Chinese suzerainty; provided for the first exchange of ministers; and opened Korea up to penetration by Japanese merchants. The court was split. Queen Min and senior members of her clan spoke for traditionalists who looked to China for support. More progressive ministers, seeing the transformation that American aid was already effecting in Japan, began to think that Korea should welcome stronger ties with the Meiji administration. Even the Daeweon-gun would be brought round to this point of view by subsequent events.

In May 1882 the Chinese statesman Li Hongzhang prompted King Gojong to conclude a treaty with the United States of America, harbouring for himself the vain hope that the United States would then support China's claim to suzerainty. In Seoul, a mutiny erupted among elements of the army opposed to the treaty and to King Gojong's request for Japanese military advice. Anti-Japanese rioting took place and the Japanese legation was burned. Both Japan and China sent troops, and the Daeweon-gun was captured and removed to China. This was China's chance to reassert its old authority, and it began by creating a branch of its own (foreign-officered) Imperial Maritime Customs Service in Korea. But Japan quickly won reparation for the crisis and stationed troops in Seoul: the stage was set for Korea to become the battleground in the looming conflict between East Asia's age-old rivals.

King Gojong saw the United States as a potential counterweight to both Japan and China, and in 1883 dispatched the Queen's nephew, Prince Min Yeong-ik, to Washington to seek American advisers. The first to arrive was the US minister Lucius Foote in 1883, joined the following year by George Foulk as naval attaché and the Rev. Dr. Horace Allen as physician to the legation. Soon treaties were signed with European countries, and foreigners of other nationalities were drawn into the Korean maelstrom. Their initial impressions could hardly have been less encouraging. On 4 December 1884 a group of modernization supporters, known as the Progressive Party (*Gaehwadang*), attempted to seize power by attacking and killing pro-Chinese members of the Min clan at a dinner celebrating the opening of the Seoul post office, at which foreign residents were present (Fig. *i.i*). By helping to save the life of the badly injured Min Yeong-ik, Horace Allen earned the King's gratitude, a development that would prove to be significant both for the acceptance of Christianity and the implantation of Western influence. The King sought sanctuary in the Japanese legation, and the Progressives demanded the return of the

i.i The Post Office, scene of the coup attempt in December 1884.

Daeweon-gun from China. Their success was short-lived, however, for Chinese troops in their turn forced Gojong back to his palace, and anti-Japanese feeling spilled onto the streets in an orgy of violence.

As his father and his wife struggled against each other to manipulate him, King Gojong vacillated. He was by nature too equivocal to cope with new challenges. He acknowledged the need for reforms and welcomed the improvements that Westerners as individuals were able to make to his people's conditions, but shied away from radical changes to the political system. He appointed foreign advisers, and towards the end of the century commentators described him as 'progressive and pro-Western' and 'one of the most urbane and gracious sovereigns that ever sat on the throne of Chosen'.

Others were less kind: the American William Sands said that he 'had no will', while the British traveller Isabella Bird Bishop said that he 'made havoc of reigning'. Events in the 1890s provide the key to such differing assessments. By then, people in the countryside were suffering widely from natural disasters, corrupt administration, over-taxation, and damage to their trade caused by the domination of Japanese merchants. Early in 1894 the **Donghak** ('Eastern Learning') **rebellion** broke out in the south-western province of Jeolla, demanding social reforms and an end to foreign intrusion. Seoul itself seemed threatened, but in early June 3,000 Chinese troops arrived and a truce was agreed. Japan, meanwhile, dispatched twice as many of its soldiers to Korea and used the crisis to advance its own influence. On 23 July Japanese troops entered the Gyeongbok Palace, imprisoned the royal family, and brought the Daeweon-gun back to power. Two days later the Japanese navy sank a British ship carrying more Chinese soldiers to Korea, and on 1 August China and Japan formally declared war on each other.

At Japanese insistence, King Gojong established a new Advisory Council under the progressive minister Gim Hongjip (Plate 3) to renounce Chinese suzerainty and to initiate immediate reforms (the so-called **Gabo reforms**). Though many of these were essential for Korean modernization, they exacerbated the tensions of an already turbulent period. The Donghak rebels took up arms again; popular resentment rose against what was widely, and correctly, interpreted as a tightening of Japan's grip on Korea; the Treaty of Shimonoseki, which followed Japan's convincing victory over China, fooled nobody when it reaffirmed Korea's independence; and in October 1895 Queen Min was assassinated in a Japanese-instigated assault. The King escaped to the safety of the Russian legation, where he rescinded the most unpopular Gabo edicts and restored a more autocratic government structure, even declaring himself Emperor in 1897. Reformist officials joined the **Independence Club**, founded in July 1896 by young nationalists including the US-educated Philip

Jaisohn (Seo Jaepil). The Club pressed the King to consider more democratic participation in government and put an end to foreign influence, but after violent fighting on the streets of Seoul it was disbanded in November 1897 and many of its leaders were imprisoned.

Westerners, who had generally welcomed the Gabo reforms, now expressed misgivings at Gojong's apparent loss of will. An editorial in *The Korean Repository* commented that 'the sky is not as bright as it might be. We have hope but we wish we had less fear.' Isabella Bishop, it is true, shrewdly anticipated Japan's ambition 'to add, for all practical purposes of commerce and emigration, a mainland province to her empire', but on the whole foreigners seemed unable to see the threat posed by Japanese imperial ambition and failed to recognize the justification for Korean distrust of Japanese control. Only Russia, whose sphere of influence in Manchuria might be challenged by the Japanese occupation of Korea, expressed serious concern. The two powers tried to regularize their respective interests, but their failure to agree contributed to the outbreak of the Russo–Japanese War in 1904, fought largely on Korean soil. The surprising ease of its emphatic victory was all Japan needed to prompt the declaration of its **Protectorate** over the peninsula in 1905, still supposedly in the name of Korean independence. There followed five years during which the Japanese, under their Resident General Ito Hirobumi, tightened their grip over many aspects of Korean life, including its financial affairs, army, education, and publishing. They compelled Emperor Gojong, who appealed in vain to the Hague Peace Conference in 1907 for genuine Korean independence, to abdicate in favour of his son, named as Emperor Sunjong. Gojong lived on in the Deoksu Palace until 1919, but Sunjong lacked even his father's minimal determination and proved no better than a puppet ruler. When, on 29 August 1910, he signed the Treaty of Japanese Annexation which had already been signed by the quisling Prime Minister Yi Wanyong, many Koreans committed suicide. Thus, ignominiously, fell the Joseon dynasty, and Seoul, as the fulcrum of Korea, entered into a period of foreign occupation which brought with it the confusing and agonizing changes shared by other colonies around the world in the early twentieth century.

1
The Setting

MODERN SEOUL IS a city of eleven million inhabitants, one of the largest in Asia and in the world. It grew to prominence in the twentieth century, but crucial to its development were the events of the last two decades of the nineteenth century. This was the time of Korea's reluctant opening up to the West, and the time when the first foreign residents strove to come to terms with what they called the 'Hermit Kingdom' because of its contented isolation from the rest of the world. They could scarcely have anticipated either the extent or the speed of the city's future transformation. Most of it, said the American medical missionary Horace Allen on his arrival in 1884, was little better than 'a collection of haystacks that have wintered out'. His compatriot Louise Miln likened its buildings to 'a bed of thriving mushrooms'. The Scot James Scarth Gale also had reservations: 'Viewed as a whole, Seoul is said to be the most picturesque city in the East; viewed in detail, it contains much to make one shudder.' But the inveterate English traveller Isabella Bishop, having referred in 1896 to 'its unspeakable meanness and faded splendors', realized a year later that 'it is entitled to be regarded as one of the great capitals of the world ... and that few capitals are more beautifully situated' (Plate 4).

To some critics, Seoul still appears to have no distinctive appearance and little soul. Its high-rise buildings and concrete flyovers proclaim its dedication to modernity and internationalism. But it treasures reminders of a glorious, if uneasy, past. The Great South and East Gates (Plate 5, Figs. 1.1 & 1.2) were built in 1398 and 1399, at the very beginning of Joseon rule. Buildings in four royal palaces date

1.1 The Great South Gate, *Illustrated London News*, 3 April 1886.

from the seventeenth century. From the nineteenth century, Myeong-dong Cathedral and Independence Arch (Plate 15) represent Korea's response to the wider world, while behind the Westin Chosun Hotel stands a single pavilion from the Altar of Heaven, built in 1897 and now a forlorn reminder of a short-lived claim to imperial sovereignty (see Chapter 3).

The name Seoul ('capital') was variously spelled by the early Westerners, as Söul and Sole among other versions, and the present form only achieved complete official recognition after World War Two. In the past the city had chiefly been known as Hanseong ('Fortress on the Han') or Hanyang ('The sunny side of Han'). It lay in a protected basin, surrounded by a ring of hills to the North and bounded by the Han river along its southern fringe. 'Where could one

1.2 Tramlines inside the Great East Gate, c.1900.

find a spot on earth richer in scenic attractions than Seoul itself and its environs? The situation of the city spread out in its basin with its grand amphitheater of granite hills is one whose artistic effect is so striking that it can never fail to produce agreeable sensations,' read an article in *The Korean Repository* in May 1892.

When the location first commended itself as the site for the new capital in 1394, it already had a history of settlement stretching back over a thousand years. Ministers argued over the need to move the capital from the previous capital at Gaeseong, but the Buddhist priest and ***peungsu*** expert Muhak ('Lacking learning'), whose advice had been sought, had read the signs well. (He may have taken into account also that the location he proposed had once been planted with plum trees, and that Yi ('plum') was the family name of his royal master, Yi Seonggye.) For more than five hundred years, the city survived all manner of misfortunes and established a complete metropolitan dominance in political, economic, social, and cultural spheres. This was perpetuated under Japanese colonial rule (1910–45) and has endured to the present, making Seoul the magnet that has attracted fame and fortune to many families. According to an old proverb, 'If you have a horse, send it to Jeju [the southern island famed for its horse-breeding]; if you have a son, send him to Seoul'. Nevertheless, the consequences of the city's pre-eminence have not always been beneficial. Because so many of the country's physical and intellectual resources were concentrated there, the destruction it suffered during the Korean War (1950–3) was devastating. Even so, in the decades of restoration that followed, the capital (now of South Korea) continued to profit at the expense of the provinces, attracting the lion's share of resources for new buildings, education, commerce, and entertainment: anybody with ambition still made for Seoul. At the beginning of the twenty-first century, one quarter of South Korea's population lived there.

The site for Yi Seonggye (now King Taejo)'s new palace (see Chapter 4) was also determined by *peungsu* diviners, though this time the decision went against Muhak's advice. A shrine to his ancestors was built on the site of the present Royal Ancestral Shrine, Jongmyo. Then came the massive granite walls of the city, forty-two feet high and nearly six miles long, which took 200,000 labourers only nine months to build and which were completed in September 1396. Their route had been empirically defined by the area left uncovered by drifts after a particularly heavy snowfall, and 'wander[ed] over the tops of hills, topped with pine, and in season ablaze with azaleas of all hues, rhododendron and plum blossom, and join[ed] a higher line of defence crowning the massive rock citadel of the Puk Han [mountain] range' (W.F. Sands). They were punctuated by eight gates, four major ones (South, North, East, and West) and four of lesser grandeur. In keeping with Chinese custom, the South Gate was the principal entrance to the city. In the late nineteenth century all were still standing, though today only the South and East Gates survive. In 1398 the Altars of Earth and Harvest and the Temple of Confucius were constructed, reflecting the early Joseon rulers' rejection of Buddhism and espousal of neo-Confucianism.

None of the maps drawn of the city before 1592 have survived. Late nineteenth-century plans (Plate 6) were often based on Gim Jeongho's *Suseon cheondo* ('Complete Map of the First and Best City'), published in 1824 and redrawn for the use of foreigners in 1885. The city was first and foremost a political and administrative centre, and headquarters for the armies and military command structure which defended it. It was divided into five sections (*pu*)—

North, South, East, West, and Centre, with the main street, Jongno, as the chief axis—which were coloured separately on early maps. In each section there was a Confucian College, the most important of which (Seonggyungwan, founded in 1398) survives to the present day. Its students were no strangers to direct action: in 1510 they tried to destroy the 'heretical' teachings of Buddhism by burning down the Hungcheon Temple, just outside the East Gate. In Korea neo-Confucianism, according to the interpretation put on it by many politicians, was far from being a homogeneous or tolerant philosophy. The five sections were subdivided into wards named *dong* ('village'), as the districts of Seoul still are today. The rise and fall in their fortunes and those of their principal **yangban** clans, occupational guilds, and political factions dominated national affairs. Their bitter, even violent, rivalry severely undermined the smooth government of the country between the sixteenth and nineteenth centuries.

Hanseong was protected not only by the city walls but also by two mountain fortresses: one, which may still be seen today, high up in the hills to its north (Bukhan Sanseong), and one in the hills beyond the Han River to the south (Namhan Sanseong). These ancient stone fortifications dated from the sixth century, when the kingdom of Baekje had its capital here, but in 1592 neither walls nor *peungsu* were able to protect Hanseong against Toyotomi Hideyoshi's soldiers. At their approach King Seonjo and his court fled north to the Chinese border; the city quickly succumbed; and almost all of its great buildings were destroyed. Less than forty years later the court was in flight again. In 1627, as the Manchus captured Pyeongyang and threatened the capital, the court withdrew to the island of Ganghwa at the mouth of the Han River. On this occasion the Manchus were bought off, but worse was to come. When King Injo refused to endorse their claim to the Chinese throne, they invaded Korea again in 1636. The Queen and other members of the royal family sought refuge once more on Ganghwa, where they were captured. The King and the Crown Prince, having remained to lead the defences, were besieged in Namhan Sanseong, and when at last it succumbed in the early days of 1637, were forced to kneel in the snow in homage to the future Manchu Son of Heaven. A stele marks the spot, inscribed in Chinese and Manchu. The Manchus, intent on the larger prize of China, allowed the Yi clan to carry on ruling.

Korea is not a big country. From top to bottom it stretches scarcely six hundred miles. Mountain ranges divide it and rivers act as barriers as well as lines of transport, yet both ancient and modern history have shown how susceptible it is to invasion from north and south alike, and have underlined the importance of effective communications between Seoul and its provinces.

Traditionally, messages were carried on horseback over poor roads, and every evening a system of beacons was lit across the land to report to the capital that all was well. The king was informed, the court orchestra played, the curfew bell was rung, and the city gates were shut until dawn. If these gates and beacons provided less sense of security to the first foreign residents of Seoul than they did to the court, yet the first missionaries were not deterred from undertaking daring journeys of exploration beyond them and into the interior. In 1887 Horace Underwood passed through Gaeseong and Pyeongyang on his way as far north as Uiju, on the Chinese border, baptizing over twenty adults before his return to Seoul. Two years later, he and his new bride, Dr Lillias Horton, spent an adventurous honeymoon travelling still further up the course of the Yalu River. Lillias, carried in a chair by two bearers, was the first Western woman to be seen in these remote areas, and her later account of her life in Korea (see Bibliography) illustrates how hard it was for these pioneers to come to terms with what they found. Though they carried safe conduct documents issued to them by the Korean government and were rarely threatened, they were apprehensive and some carried guns. One of the first to work in Pyeongyang, known to some missionaries as 'the Sodom of Korea', was the American Methodist William Hall. Some of his converts were imprisoned, tortured, and stoned for assisting him to buy property, but it took a major battle there between Chinese and Japanese armies during the Sino–Japanese war in 1894 to drive him out. When he returned three weeks later he found the streets full of dead and decaying bodies. He stayed on for a month, suffering from malaria, but died in Seoul after contracting typhus on the ship that brought him back via Jemulpo (modern Incheon), leaving a widow and two young children.

As mission stations and commercial installations extended beyond Seoul as far as Uiju on the Chinese border and Busan on the south coast, foreigners felt isolated and sometimes in danger. They needed up-to-date links with the outside world, and new technologies gradually signalled the end of an era. The telegraph was introduced and by 1898 nine offices had opened across the country, eclipsing the beacons and creating direct links with China and Europe. The postal service between Seoul and Jemulpo, which carried twelve letters on its inaugural delivery on 23 July 1895 and 616 in its first month, 'was likewise growing in favour with the people', according to *The Korean Repository* in January 1898. And then came the railway.

'Seoul is a pleasant place to live in for ten months of the year. July and August are excepted', wrote *The Korean Repository*'s editor in June 1896. The following summer, fifty inches of rain (double the average amount) led to disastrous crops of apples, pears, peaches, and nectarines, associated with plagues of aphids, beetles, caterpillars, and wasps. At such times, when the dampness caused 'weariness, general prostration and frequently severe sickness', foreigners dreamed of being able to leave Seoul in search of pleasanter rural conditions. A railway would make a lot of difference. In March 1896 a US syndicate under James Morse won a concession to build the first line, from Seoul to Jemulpo, and work began in December. Seoul railway station, 'a handsome frame building with a brick foundation', was built in sections at Chattanooga in the US state of Tennessee and shipped across the Pacific. It was assembled outside the West Gate, the 'picturesque double-roofed gateway of the Gate of Staunch Loyalty which make[s] the western entrance to the Korean capital so unique and attractive' (Isabella Bishop). In 1901 *The Korea Review* enthused, 'Five trains a day each way should be enough to satisfy even the most impetuous of us.' The train took around two hours to travel the twenty-six miles, as compared with six hours by chair. Horace Allen, an 'expert bicyclist', cycled it in three hours and fourteen minutes.

The introduction of the telegraph, postal service, and railway revolutionized physical communication between the capital and provincial towns. No less significant in spreading information and ideas was the arrival of modern journalism. The Japanese helped to produce the first newspapers in the1880s. At first they were printed in a mixture of Chinese characters and Korean *hangeul* script and had a limited readership, but towards the end of the 1890s Korean nationalists realized their importance, and of several new titles the most influential was Seo Jaepil's *Dongnip Sinmun* ('Independent News'), first printed on 7 April 1896. Mrs Bishop said that 'among the novelties of 1897 is the sight of newsboys passing through the streets with bundles of a newspaper in *En-mun* [*hangeul*] under their arms, and of men reading them in the shops.'

2

The Inhabitants

In 1669 THE population of Seoul numbered around 194,000. A surviving census register of its northern section in 1663 divides its population of some 2,400, drawn from 681 households, into members of the 'exalted' (*hyeon*) gentry class known as *yangban*, the 'cultivators' (*jak*) or commoners of the *sangmin* ('common people') class, and private and government **slaves**. Around 16.6 per cent of the households belonged to yangban families, 30 per cent to sangmin, and a massive 53.3 per cent to slaves. Over the next two hundred years this composition changed little, and by 1901 the number of inhabitants, occupying 42,565 houses, had only risen to 196,898. Of these the yangban still constituted a minority, while the majority of the remainder belonged to sangmin households. Traditionally, sangmin pursued occupations associated with farming, labouring, and soldiery, but the rise in specialized production of consumer goods and commerce from the late eighteenth century onwards produced merchant families whose wealth and affluent lifestyles so stretched the composition of the sangmin that their former identification as 'common people' became inappropriate.

The yangban were educated in classical Chinese, studied the Classics of Confucianism, and were promoted up the official ladder by passing Chinese-style examinations. As the social elite, many of them possessed country estates on which they preferred to live as masters of village communities when they were not occupying government positions in Seoul. They admired and imitated many aspects of Chinese culture. Their court rituals and principles of government were modelled on those of Beijing, and their patterns and rules of social behaviour conformed conscientiously to Confucian standards. They adhered strictly to the precepts of filial piety: the duties owed by the younger generation to its elders; a son to his father and grandfather; an inferior to his professional superior; a wife to her husband; and, by extension, a vassal state to its suzerain. The men prostrated themselves before the tablets of their departed ancestors. When they visited each other's homes they discussed poetry, calligraphy, and philosophy as well as the latest gossip from court ('Korea is the country of wild rumours', said Isabella Bishop).

However, gentry lifestyle and taste were not simply the mirror images of the Chinese that they appeared to be (Plate 7). As the Joseon dynasty wore on, both men and women made increasing use of Korea's own *hangeul* alphabet in addition to and instead of Chinese characters. Korean painting, poetry, and music included forms that had evolved from native as well as Chinese traditions. The artist Gim Heongdo (1745–post-1814) is the most popular today of those who could paint both in authentic Chinese style and also with a quite distinctive Korean feel (Plate 8).

Koreans were also proud of their own dress styles. Within the yangban class differences of grade, representing levels of official post held, were marked by styles of dress and ornaments. At court, the king and his civil and military officials wore a colourful variety of robes, belts, footwear, and headgear for different purposes. Rank was also indicated by Korean versions of the Chinese mandarin squares, decorated panels worn on the chest and back. For everyday wear, styles were simpler. Men wore loose fitting trousers and a long robe with wide sleeves (see Fig. 3.10). Women wore thin trousers under a long, high-waisted skirt that covered the up-turned toes of their shoes, and a short jacket with fairly tight sleeves. If they had to go out in public, however, they wore the *jangot*, a cape with an integral hood that concealed their features (see Fig. 3.5). As a minor concession to modernization the Daeweon-gun ordered simplifications in dress in 1871, including a narrowing of men's sleeves, but the changes—though comparatively minor—were not generally popular. To a Korean, his dress was part of his character. 'The Corean man specially prides himself on the spotless purity and lustre of his white clothing', reported Louise Miln. In summer clothes were washed whole, in winter they were taken to pieces to be washed, and for New Year visiting new clothes were worn if possible. 'So poor and proud are the Coreans that when they come to Soul they hire fashionable clothes in which to swagger through the streets of the capital.'

An important rite of passage for every teenage boy, whether of yangban or sangmin class, was his 'capping' as an adult, just before his marriage. Thereafter his hair remained uncut and tied up in a topknot (*sangtu*), of which all men were immensely proud. A tight headband of lacquered horsehair (*mangen*) kept it in place, and rings behind the ears denoted the wearer's rank, the first three being of jade for the first class, gold for the second, and silver for the third. Sangmin men wore rings of bone, horn, or shell. A tall, broad-rimmed hat made of split bamboo, also lacquered, was assumed at the same time, with buttons of jade or crystal, according to rank, where the chinstrap was attached. In the name of modernization, an ill-judged attempt was made in 1895 to compel men to give up their treasured horsehair hats. Still worse, the simultaneous order that men should cut off their topknots led to near riots. One father whose sons obeyed the command committed suicide. As farmers who disobeyed it stayed safely away from the authorities in Seoul, food prices there rose. Before long King Gojong rescinded the order, restoring men's right to dress how they wished.

As a class the yangban may only have comprised a small percentage of the population, but they owned substantial amounts of land and considerable numbers of tenant farmers and slaves in Seoul and across Korea, and generally lived in far grander conditions than the sangmin. Even so, neither the job security of an individual nor the prosperity of his family was guaranteed. Some scholars accepted penury as the price for a life of literary composition or for defending unpopular political principles. Entire clans might find their social status put in jeopardy by royal disfavour, political rivalry with other clans, or simple economic misfortune. Impeachment for genuine or trumped-up misdemeanours could bring swift disgrace. For an official convicted of a light offence, the punishment might be no more than temporary dispatch back to his native town or to a village outside Seoul, but those condemned for serious crimes were exiled to a far region, usually an island such as Jeju, where they were imprisoned within a thorn hedge, described as 'a living death'. The most degrading form of punishment was the chain-gang in which three or four culprits were yoked by the neck, dressed in blue uniform, given dirty jobs to do, and mocked through the streets. Until 1894, retribution was also taken against a felon's family.

Upward mobility into the yangban class was almost impossible through the early Joseon period, as it depended upon passing examinations which were beyond the reach of the lower classes. However, by the late nineteenth century the dividing lines between social classes were growing more blurred. Over the previous hundred years yangban had been forging agreements with merchants or owners of craft workshops to try and revive their fortunes, and the arrival of the Westerners created new opportunities for money-making and lucrative joint ventures. Now, those meriting upper class status on authentic educational criteria became hardly distinguishable from those using their wealth simply to adopt upper class *mores*. Even at the other end of the scale, change was admitted. In response to a plea submitted to the Home Department by a Christian butcher, members of that trade, traditionally regarded as social pariahs, were given permission for the first time in July 1895 to wear the wide sleeves of normal male dress, the topknot band, and the horsehair hat, which qualified them to be addressed conversationally as men rather than boys. People were now expressly forbidden to beat them.

Judging by the 1663 census register perhaps three-quarters of the Seoul population was then enslaved, either to the government or to yangban households. By the late nineteenth century the number had fallen to about one in twenty, most of them female. Slavery had become largely indistinguishable from many other forms of service status, and in 1884 the first US legation was housed in a rather grand building purchased from a wealthy slave, Gim Gamjeok. The Gabo reforms officially abolished slavery, along with child marriage, the ban on the remarrying of widows, and the torture of suspected criminals, but the social habits and attitudes of centuries took time to change. The popular Independence Club still felt the need to debate the issue in November 1897, and almost one hundred slaves were afterwards set free.

Changes in the legal, political, economic, military, and educational systems all began to gather pace. In 1898 the

Official Gazette reported that instructions had been issued against **shamans** befouling the streets with refuse and smoking the yard-long pipes 'over which the men will squat for hours in front of their houses' (Plate 10). New rules on improving conditions in gaols were also published. *The Korean Repository* commented wryly that 'the Department [of Justice] has issued such orders before, but they were not enforced through various unfortunate causes.' Nevertheless, as the century drew to a close the paper's editor found grounds for optimism about the social situation: 'The street beggars seen in Japan and China are absent in Korea for the reason that the humblest Korean generally has some place of refuge from starvation. Poverty there is but not want.'

Amid these changes the position of women was not seriously questioned. As in traditional China, Korean women were hidden away in the 'inner quarters' of the household, jealously guarded against prying eyes. Pre-pubescent siblings lived and played together, but by the age of twelve a girl must be shut away in the female apartments, forbidden to see any males other than relatives down to her fourth cousins (the 'eighth joint'), even eating her meals separately, until she married. (Unnatural as this might seem, it meant that she could nonetheless know up to two hundred men and boys.) Until the Gabo reforms raised the minimum age for this vital rite of passage to sixteen, it not uncommonly took place around the age of ten, and was arranged through the services of a professional matchmaker. It was a serious matter to be still unmarried by the age of twenty. At least Korean girls were spared the cruel Chinese custom of foot-binding, but if they had reason to venture beyond the home, to visit friends for example, yangban women were supposed to do so within a tightly curtained box chair. By the late nineteenth century, however, more and more women of all classes were literally

16

taking to their feet, concealed within a *jangot*, to pursue outside occupations as girls' tutor, physician, shopkeeper, matchmaker, wet nurse, washerwoman, domestic or palace servant, cook, or **gisaeng**. An open day at Ihwa school (see Chapter 5) in May 1896 attracted 657 women.

Parents were often disappointed by the birth of a girl rather than a boy, though the writings of Lady Hyegyeong, born into a yangban family in 1735, stress how greatly she and her sister were loved. Like other women, she wrote in *hangeul* rather than Chinese characters, which were a male prerogative. Not all women were condemned to illiteracy by their menfolk, but the idea of school education for girls was a radical innovation which provoked considerable hostility when foreign missions began to promote it in the 1880s. Often treated as no more than possessions, women accepted that although a man might legally take only one wife, he was free to introduce any number of concubines into his household. Christian missionaries might rail against polygamy, indeed *The Korean Repository* in 1895 urged the Presbyterian church to exclude those who practised it, but to the yangban, continuation of the male lineage was essential and the birth of sons was therefore of paramount importance. The king took concubines to ensure this, and so might his subjects.

By no means all of them did: among the sangmin in particular, economic circumstances generally safeguarded the sole position of the wife. Nor were her responsibilities within the home insignificant. In addition to the upbringing of young children and supervision of the kitchen, she had charge over the family's daily finances. In poorer households, she contributed to the needs of the family by weaving, taking in laundry, and assuming the role of the domestic shaman, performing ceremonies to the spirits that lived in the courtyard, on the roof, in the kitchen, and in the privy. Her intercessions might contribute to the success of her husband in his job and guard her family against sickness. Isabella Bishop found little to her liking in the situation of Korean women, but concluded that 'I am far from saying that [they] fret and groan under this system, or crave the freedom which European women enjoy. ... One intelligent woman, when I pressed her hard to say what they thought of our customs in the matter, replied, "We think that your husbands don't care for you very much!"'.

Professional shamans were also prominent in community affairs, especially in Seoul, where there were reported to be around one thousand in 1897. Their fees were high and their social status low, but so necessary were their services that they were patronized by all classes and the poor would even pawn their clothes to hire them. They communicated with the departed and worshipped the spirits dwelling in the mountains and seas, and prayed for good fortune in the coming year, peace, successful harvests, rest for wandering souls who had suffered sudden death, and protection against wild animals. They drove away the evil spirits of sickness and would exorcize a well in which a person had died. Christian missionaries decried their 'noisy little temples' outside the walls, but admitted that their coloured banners of paper or silk and the umbrellas and fans used in their rituals were 'expensively made and gorgeously painted' (Plate 9).

Perhaps it was because Seoul had been out of bounds to Buddhist monks for almost five hundred years that Louise Miln, discounting what the Western missionaries regarded as the superstitious pretensions of shamanism, claimed that 'of all civilized countries, Korea is the one country without a religion'. Even so, two Buddhist temples, Yeong-am and

Hungcheon, operated just outside the West and East Gates, and Lillias Underwood reported more honestly that 'women and children, and all the more ignorant, still worship and believe, to some extent.'

Life expectancy was not high: endemic diseases such as smallpox, cholera, typhoid, malaria, tuberculosis, and syphilis affected residents of the palaces and hovels alike, and were exacerbated by poor sanitary conditions and, in the opinion of some foreigners, a predilection for drink and a bias against washing. For their part, Koreans were not slow to appreciate the benefits brought by the medical missionaries, though many refused operations under anaesthesia. A cholera hospital was opened near the East Gate after an outbreak in September 1895, but was closed when 135 of its patients died; another, outside the West Gate and known as 'the Shelter', enjoyed somewhat better fortune.

For the yangban, funerary rites were elaborate, expensive, and time-consuming, and mourning observations detailed and demanding. A corpse might await burial for up to three months, sealed in an airtight pine coffin. The poor, however, could not afford such delay, and buried their deceased by the ninth day after death. No burials were allowed within the city, and corpses could only be carried out through the Little West Gate and the Watermouth Gate. Since they were shut by curfew at 9 p.m., in times of epidemic 'these gates are thronged with one stream of funeral processions'. The remains of the assassinated Queen Min found no final resting place for over five years. In April 1901 those responsible for choosing a suitable tomb site outside the East Gate were arrested, tortured, and sentenced to life imprisonment when it proved to have too much subsoil rock. Unlike Muhak, not all geomancers attained lasting fame for their decisions.

Every year a handful of men and boys died as a result of

stone fighting. During the first moon the inhabitants of one village would line up across the bare fields to chase and hurl rocks at those of another, cheered on by crowds of spectators and wreaking damage on people and buildings alike in their pursuit. In the first moon of 1905 the Seoul tram system carried twice its monthly average of passengers, suggesting that up to 25,000 people went to watch the spectacle. Police might try to intervene if things got too badly out of hand, but with little success. Lillias Underwood believed that neighbourhoods used these annual outbursts of pent-up winter energy to settle local grievances, but perhaps no such rational justification was needed for a curiously popular observance. She herself was caught up in a fight and, 'reckless of my best gown', scaled a wall with great alacrity and ran shamelessly away.

More harmless were other traditional games and forms of entertainment. Children played blind man's buff, hide-and-seek, battledore and shuttlecock, arm-wrestling, and cat's cradle. The fifteenth day of the first moon was the favourite day for the exuberant Korean form of see-sawing and the fifth day of the fifth moon for swinging, even though Korean swings were so high that accidents were common. Kite-flying was popular, and chess, cards, dominoes, and backgammon all provided opportunities for gambling (Plate 10). Despite anti-gambling laws, J. Shirley reported to the Australian Association for the Advancement of Science in 1895 that Koreans 'are born gamblers and never lose an opportunity of indulging in the practice.' Their backsliding was encouraged by the fact that the Japanese community could 'open gambling dens with impunity.' Westerners describing Korea and its people's activities to their friends and readers back home found the pictures by one man especially to their liking. His name was Gim Jun-geun, better known by his brush-name Gisan. Little is known about him today, but he was particularly successful at earning commissions in the late nineteenth century and hundreds of his charming sketches are now preserved in museums around the world (see Plates 9, 10, & 14).

Quite different in character are **'nectar paintings'** from Buddhist temples (Plate 11). Among other details these show some of the open-air entertainments provided by the bands of travelling players known as *gwangdae*. They included masked dance plays, acrobatics, and tightrope walking, all accompanied by music. While they were deservedly popular among ordinary people, scholars professed scorn for folk music and interest in a more refined musical culture. They preferred to escape from the daily routine into *pungnyu*, a relaxed enjoyment of classical music, poetry, and female companionship. However, the commercial expansion of Seoul through the nineteenth century demanded increasingly varied forms of entertainment. Contests were held in the dramatic musical story-telling form *pansori*, for which even the yangban developed a taste, hiring singers to perform at private parties, sponsoring public performances, and even learning to practise the art for themselves (Plate 12).

A few Westerners also admitted with some surprise to liking Korean music: 'I do not know how or why I like music of this kind, but it takes me away from my natal civilization' (George Foulk). It is 'to the average European ear more than diabolical, this being to a large extent due to the differences in the tones, semi-tones and intervals of the scale, but personally, having got accustomed to their tunes, I rather like its weirdness and originality' (A. H. Savage Landor). Music of a more familiar kind was made by Franz Eckert, a Prussian who arrived on 19 February 1901 to form an imperial band in Seoul after twenty years' similar service in Tokyo.

Western music had probably been heard for the first time in Seoul less than twenty years before, when Paul-Georg von Möllendorff, Chief Commissioner of Maritime Customs, engaged the band of the visiting German ship *Leipzig* to play, but the Korean band gave its first performance after only four months' practice on the unfamiliar foreign instruments.

3

Buildings and Streets

HORACE ALLEN CALLED them haystacks, Louise Miln called them mushrooms. Four centuries earlier, Chinese ambassador Dong Yue had likened them to stacks of grain, saying that poor people built their houses of mud and stones held together by ropes buried in the walls and that weeds grew alongside vegetables on the old thatched roofs (Plate 13). In every house, he said, there was a window facing north for ventilation, and the homes of the literati had 'unartistic' pictures pasted on the walls. He also said that householders had little interest in flowers (which was not the impression of Homer Hulbert, who wrote in 1906 that 'there is hardly a hut in Korea where no flower is found'), and he might as well have added that the yangban were more likely to have tiled roofs.

Further details about housing also came from Hulbert, who lived in Korea for twenty-one years: 'You will not go far along any street in Seoul without seeing houses propped up with stout sticks to stop them falling over. This is because the [heavy] roof rests solely upon tie-beams of great thickness morticed into the tops of the vertical pillars without any trusses, and even the pillars don't have proper foundations.' Floors were raised above ground level. They were made of earth and stone, through which flues carried hot air and gases from the fireplace in the kitchen. Faced in cement with a covering of strong waxed paper, this *ondol* (underfloor heating system) had provided warmth for well over a thousand years. It was comfortable and helped to account for the fact that Koreans normally sat and slept on the floor.

Every day queues of bullock- and pony-drawn carts loaded with wood and grass for household fires lined the streets (Fig. 3.1), but a heavy smoke pall hung over the city and aggravated bronchial troubles. In Seoul a man's fuel bill might burn up almost a quarter of his salary. After exceptional summer rains in 1891, a cattle epidemic killed off many of the bullocks which normally hauled the fuel carts up from Jemulpo. The result was a winter fuel crisis in the city. In 1901, too, cases of hypothermia were reported among those who could not afford the high prices of fuel.

Every house, however humble, was surrounded by a wall or a fence, partly for security but mainly to conceal the women inside from prying eyes. For the same reason, the law required a householder to inform his neighbour if he intended to climb up onto the roof of his house, lest he catch an unexpected glimpse of them. Doors were low and narrow, windows covered with white paper. Sangmin homes might have only one or two rooms, but the larger compounds of the well-to-do, said Hulbert, were a 'veritable labyrinth of numberless gates and alleys', with separate quarters for the women. The best accommodation, that of the men, was sited away from the road, but 'you will find the most horribly offensive conditions as readily among the residences of the wealthy and powerful as among the poor.' The cesspool might have to be crossed to enter the main gate, and the night soil collector was liable to be encountered coming out of the gentleman's courtyard. Lillias Underwood found 'everything in connection with these houses fearfully unsanitary, and many of them filthy and full of vermin. All sewage flows out into the unspeakable ditches on either side of the street' (Fig. 3.2).

Until 1901, when the first water was filtered and piped into the city from the Han River by an American company,

3.1 Dealers selling oak firewood.

3.2 An open drain running through a side street.

water came mainly from wells. Some yangban households had their own, but commoners had to make do with communal neighbourhood wells. Washerwomen squatted next to them, muddying the water source again as they worked. Many households relied on supplies brought to them by water carriers balancing two buckets on a shoulder-pole. Three or four such loads a day were commonplace, and bigger households might use up to twenty a day. The sewage ditches fed into a number of broad canals that ran through the city, crossed by forty bridges including six constructed of fine marble. On the fifteenth night of the first moon crowds filled the moonlit streets to observe a custom said to date back to mediaeval times, that of walking over as many bridges as possible to ward off foot trouble and other bad luck in the coming year. Yangban men would have done it two nights before, but women only did it on the following night, the sixteenth night of the first moon.

The foremost building complexes, hidden behind high walls, were the royal palaces (see Chapter 4), of which the most important, Gyeongbok and Changdeok, were both situated in the northern half of the city. A straight road leading south from the main gate of Gyeongbok was lined with the principal government buildings and connected with Jongno ('Bell Street') (Fig. 3.3). At the western end of this, the main east–west thoroughfare, stood the Gyonghui palace, and at its far end the East Gate. Less than half way along came the intersection with Namdaemunno ('Great South Gate Street'), the south–north artery that curved away down to the city's main entrance. At their junction was the eponymous bell, cast in 1396 and hanging in a belfry (*Boshingak*) (Fig. 3.10), 'the tower of the city where the roads join from the four points. It calls on men to rest, to rise, to work, to play' (Dong Yue). Every day thirty-three strokes rang

3.3 Jongno, c.1900.

1. Chae Yong-shin (1850–1941), *King Gojong,* AD 1913.

2. *Queen Min*, a portrait based on contemporary descriptions by Kwon Oh-chang (b.1948).

3. *Gim Hongjip in formal attire,* a portrait by Kwon
Oh-chang based on a late Joseon photograph.

4. *Seoul 1898, looking north from the American legation,* by the Dutch American artist Hubert Vos (1855–1935).

5. The Great South Gate of Seoul, now dwarfed by high rise buildings, National Treasure no. 1.

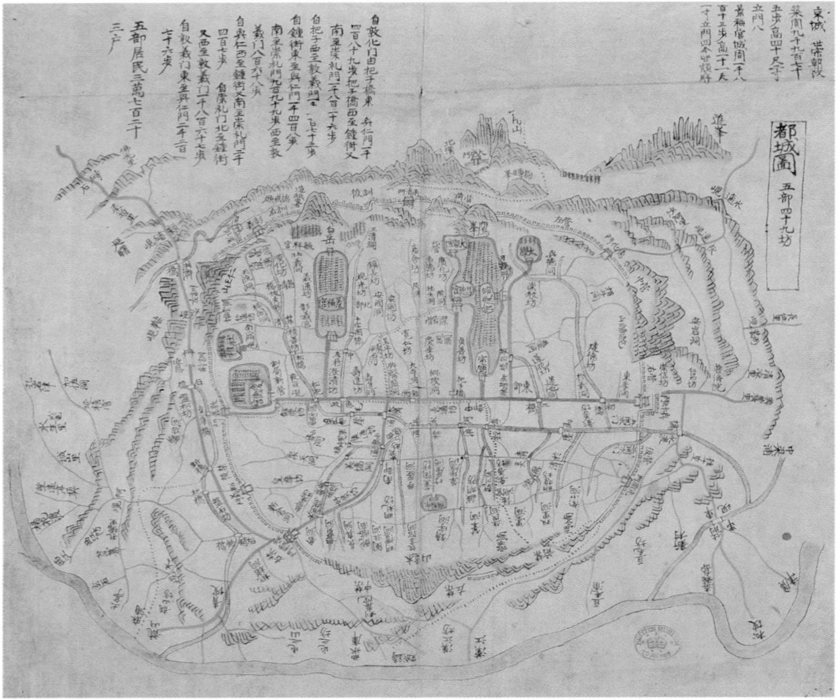

6. Street map of Seoul, anonymous, 19th century.

7.   Modern reconstruction of a scholar's studio.

8.   Gim Heongdo, *Scholar with lute*.

9. Gisan, *Shaman.*

10. Gisan, *Chess players.*

11. Monks' cymbal dance: detail from a nectar painting on the walls of Yeong-am Temple, Seoul, AD 1865.

12. *Pansori* performance: detail from a screen decorated with a view of Pyeongyang Castle, 19th century.

13. Modern reconstruction of a traditional thatched roof house.

14. Gisan, *Official on a monocycle*.

15. The Independence Arch, Seoul.

16. Hyangweon Pavilion, Gyeongbok Palace.

17. A corner of Queen Min's apartments in Gyeongbok Palace where she is said to have been assassinated.

18. The main audience hall in Deoksu Palace.

19. The corner of a roof in Changdeok Palace. The supporting timbers are painted in *dancheong*.

20. Pavilion overlooking Bandoji (Peninsula Pond) in the Secret Garden, Changdeok Palace.

21. The Royal Ancestral Shrine: the annual rite honouring the spirits of the Yi royal clan.

22. The present descendant of Emperor Sunjong dressed in the ceremonial robes of the late Joseon court.

23. Party held in 1809 to celebrate the 60th anniversary of Queen Hyegyeong's marriage.

24. Detail of a *uigwe* screen painting, AD 1902.

out over the city at dawn and twenty-eight at dusk, as guards called out to announce the opening and closing of the city gates.

After the curfew only women were allowed on the streets, but this law was falling into abeyance by the late nineteenth century and after 12 April 1895 the daily ringing of the bell was moved to noon. By then, the streets had become so badly clogged by the erection of stalls and shopfront extensions that the central carriageway was too narrow and overcrowded. When the king was due to pass by in procession, an elaborate and brilliant spectacle witnessed by tens of thousands of silent onlookers, many had to be taken down. It came as a relief when in September 1896 the adviser to the Treasury, John McLeavey Brown, ordered the clearing of temporary booths and the widening of main roads to fifty-five feet, along with a general clean-up of the drainage system. New booths 'of uniform façade, nine feet high, roofed with any material other than thatch, may by license be erected for a period of ten years on spare ground beyond the roadway' (Fig. 3.4). To those newly arrived Westerners who still expressed their dislike of conditions in Seoul, Mrs Scranton said that they could scarcely appreciate the difference the last ten years had made, and *The Korean Repository* commented that 'street improvements continued throughout the whole year and at the present rate of progress we shall be ready for horseless carriages in a short time, if our enthusiasm is not chilled or checked.'

In keeping with their Confucian outlook the early Joseon rulers had strictly regulated commerce, which was traditionally conducted nationally through a system of regional and local markets. A handful of provincial market towns had always been important social and economic centres. Daegu, for example, attracted buyers from far and

3.4 A stall selling domestic hardware, including pipe-stems.

wide for its medicinal herbs, and by the late eighteenth century its population rivalled that of Seoul at around 200,000. In the capital, only merchants licensed to retail the key commodities of cotton cloth, ramie, woollen goods, silk, paper, and marine produce were officially permitted to trade. They were known as the 'Six Licensed Shops': the government leased them sites in prime positions along the main roads; controlled weights, measures, and prices in their stores; and accepted their rents in kind.

In the late eighteenth century agricultural productivity rose and a commercial revolution began to undermine these monopolies. Even yangban and soldiers flouted the law. The number of licensed premises increased fourfold to around 120 and the government benefited from their fiscal revenue, but as the population of Seoul increased and diversified into manufacturing its need for food and clothing multiplied proportionately. The profits from commerce were so attractive that illegal markets operated near the main gates and unauthorized merchants stimulated the development of the small settlements of Yeongsan, Mabo, Yihyeon, and Sogang in the country between the southern perimeter of the city wall and the banks of the Han River.

King Jeongjo often met merchants to hear their concerns, and in 1786 the demand for currency forced the government to mint new coinage. In 1892 the mint was moved out of Seoul ('the noisiest affair the capital has witnessed for many a year') to Jemulpo and put under Japanese control, but foreigners complained that the metal currency was heavy and of little value: nine pounds (lbs) of cash were worth about one shilling. When new copper and silver coins were introduced in 1895 they were deemed a great improvement, although in 1906, according to Hulbert, barter was still the principal method of commercial exchange.

The main streets were lined with shops and stalls, as well as mats and trays on which street vendors set out their wares. The better shops were to be found around the belfry intersection on Jongno, selling poultry, beef, eggs, rice, vegetables (turnips and lettuce), and footwear (Fig. 3.5). Mrs Scranton wrote in 1896 that 'Beef was forbidden, on account of disease among the cattle ... But there were chickens and eggs ... In outward appearance these resembled those we call by the name in the home land, [but] the taste we thought as different as the two countries themselves. But we ate them ... until they came out at our nostrils.'

Other foreigners found the range of goods limited and prices high. David Spencer, newly arrived from Japan in November 1896, lamented that children's toys were not to be had. However, at Christmas 1901 the *Korea Review*

3.5 A rice shop. The woman on the right is wearing a jangot.

3.6 An apothecary's shop, with typically divided windows.

reported that 'the public has been privileged to witness a very pretty display of Christmas toys at L. Rondon's new store near the palace. Life-size dolls in ravishing frocks are reinforced with piles of bonbons, enough to satisfy the most capacious holiday appetite.' Shops selling metal pipes and tobacco boxes were social centres where men sat to hear novels read. People also gathered at drugstores, which sold traditional remedies made, according to the American Dr Busteed, from woodlice, worms, grey spiders, dung beetles, and other unattractive ingredients. They were concentrated around the South Gate, marked by 'paper windows with smaller windows in the centre of them, kept ajar by little sticks' (Fig. 3.6).

As the commercial and international status of Seoul increased, eating and drinking establishments proliferated between the South Gate and Jongno to cater for the growing number of travellers arriving from Jemulpo and the provinces. Brothels flourished outside the South Gate, but it was said that you could not find an inn in the city because there was no demand for them: any visitor would have an introduction to somebody willing to provide him with accommodation. Sights along the streets were put there to encourage the virtuous and deter miscreants. 'Banner gates', painted red and bearing an inscription praising the recipient, were sometimes erected across the street on government orders to reward loyal subjects, faithful widows, and self-sacrificing exemplars of filial piety. One had been put up in 1758 to honour Princess Hwasun, who starved herself to death when her husband Lord Weolsong died. By contrast, foreigners such as Mrs Bishop and William Sands were shocked in 1894 and again in 1898 to see the severed heads of Donghak rebels hanging by their hair from tripods made of sticks, played with by children and gnawed at by dogs. Mangy dogs roamed freely, pursued by the dog butcher, and there were reports of passers-by being attacked by mad dogs. In a superstitious attempt to deter them, people would not feed them on the morning of New Year's day.

As in any conurbation, street safety in Seoul sometimes fell victim to political and economic crises. Following the Post Office coup attempt in December 1884 mobs roamed the streets, stoned the Japanese legation, ransacked the homes of pro-Japanese ministers, and murdered the would-be Prime Minister Hong Yeongsik. The homes of the American advisers George Foulk and Walter Townsend were looted, and most foreign residents fled in terror to the US legation. On 11 February 1896 Prime Minister Gim Hongjip (Plate 3) and Minister of Agriculture Jeong Pyeongha, identified as the chief architects of the generally unpopular Gabo reforms, were publicly beheaded on Jongno and their naked bodies given to the demonstrating crowds for bloodthirsty vengeance. Ironically, the reforms included the introduction of a police force, generally regarded as efficient; the substitution of strangulation or poisoning (one means of which was by ingesting boiled centipede) for beheading in capital cases; the (nominal) abolition of torture; and improvements to gaols. In 1897 Mrs Bishop, though finding the police 'overpaid and untrustworthy', pronounced that 'the great Seoul prison contrasts most favourably with the prisons of China and other unreformed Oriental countries.' Yet public safety continued to be problematic. The summer drought in 1901 led to food shortages and a rise in street crime. Highway robbery increased, and the streets were deemed unsafe for foreigners after dark, despite the appointment of special night watchmen who went around ringing bells.

Among the beneficiaries of partially improved road conditions were foreign bicyclists, seven in number in 1896, of whom four were female, whose progress around the city on two wheels caused the local people either amusement or fright. Within two years the numbers of bicycles in use throughout Korea had swelled to around one hundred, most of them made in the United States and Japan. Veiled women, said *The Korean Repository*, were particularly likely to be run over, but potholes and ruts were universal and made cycling hazardous for riders as well. According to Hulbert, anyone who needed mud or plaster to mend a wall or smoke-flue would simply go and dig it up from the middle of the road.

So uneven were the streets that Koreans preferred to be carried around rather than trust in wheels. Until 1895 senior officials were still to be seen perched on a monocycle, supported by three footmen (Plate 14), but the usual mode of transport for those who could afford it was the palanquin or covered chair (Fig. 3.7). Chairs could be hired from ranks

3.7 Mrs Lucius Foote carried in a diplomatic palanquin.

(600 cash for ten Korean miles), though most yangban possessed their own. Upper class women rode in covered box chairs, 'distinguished by fan-shaped bangles hanging in rows on the sides,' with curtains concealing them from the sight of passers-by. Koreans and foreigners alike rode on mules, and merchants' carts trundled up to the city gates drawn by horse or the invaluable buffalo. But it was the human porter who was the most ubiquitous carrier of heavy loads, the A-frame on his back piled high with wood, vegetables, fish, seaweed, bamboo, paper, or pots and pans (Fig 3.8). It was said that a man could lift up to 250 lbs with ease and 300 lbs with assistance. With 100 lbs on his back he could average thirty miles a day.

3.8 Pedlar carrying chickens on an A-frame. (Such a picture may have been posed.)

In 1898 a group of Koreans and Americans set up the Seoul Electric Company (Fig. 3.9) with a plan to light the streets. At the same time, the company building the Jemulpo to Seoul railway, Henry Collbran and Harry Bostwick's American Oriental Construction Company, won the contract to build an electric tramcar system from the proposed Seoul railway station to the East Gate via the South Gate and Jongno. Both companies would derive their electricity from a power plant near the East Gate. US Minister Horace Allen performed the ground-breaking ceremony for the 'electric street railway' on 7 September 1898, and both lighting and tramcars were in operation in May 1899 (Fig. 3.10). Opposition came from *peungsu* experts who claimed that the overhead wires caused that year's drought; from accident victims who had been

3.9 Headquarters of the Seoul Electric Company, near the East gate.

3.10 Passengers boarding a tramcar at the Belfry. Notice the people-catcher on the front of the tram.

sleeping on the lines, using the rails for pillows, and had somehow escaped the 'people-catcher' nets hung on the front of the cars; from nationalists who objected to the employment of Japanese as drivers; and from disgruntled chair-carriers who saw their livelihood threatened. Violence erupted and employees were injured, even though the company tried to defuse tension by setting up a moving picture theatre (entrance, 3 cents) and hiring acrobats to perform at the terminus. On 1 November 1901 the frequency of trams was increased from twenty minutes to ten minutes along the nine miles of track.

In January 1901 the *Korea Review* published a résumé of the great improvements that had been achieved in the previous twenty years. It referred to the construction of new roads, especially in the vicinity of the South Gate and the

Deoksu Palace, and said that 'in the matter of building, great and laudable activity has been shown.' Foreigners had not been allowed to live within the walls until King Gojong designated Jong-dong as a mission area in 1884. Then, their initial practice was to acquire and adapt suitable Korean properties, as they did for the American legation and for Horace Allen's first hospital (see Chapter 5). Gradually, however, Western architecture began to appear. The three-storeyed French legation in Jong-dong and the two-storey Japanese consulate on nearby Namsan ('an ornament to the heart of the city') were generally agreed to be outstanding examples. Standing on the main hill in Jong-dong, the Russian legation became a focal point for foreign diplomatic interest following the King's flight there in February 1895 (see Chapter 4). It had a guard of eighty marines, whereas, complained Isabella Bishop, the British 'legation gate is kept by an old Korean porter, by no means clean, lodged in a reed beehive or enlarged dog-kennel.'

The Joseon ban on Buddhism within the walls of Seoul meant the absence of that most typical architectural feature of most East Asian towns, the pagoda. The one exception, however, was notable. The great stone pagoda, still to be admired in Pagoda Park in downtown Seoul, was, in Hulbert's opinion, 'the most ancient, as well as the most notable architectural work in this city of wood and clay'. Sent from China as a gift from a Chinese emperor to his daughter when she married a Korean king, perhaps in the twelfth century, its thirteen storeys rose like a lighthouse over the surrounding townscape. It was 'slightly discoloured with age, but enough of its former purity remained to bring it into effective contrast with the sombre gray of the houses' (P. Lowell). Also imposing, but in much heavier neo-gothic style, was the Roman Catholic Cathedral in Myeong-dong. Begun in 1892 and dedicated six years later to the Immaculate Conception, it could accommodate up to three thousand worshippers.

Other Christian churches included the Anglican Church of the Advent and the 'beautiful gothic' Methodist church, with separate wings for men and women, both in Jong-dong (Fig. 3.11). There too Mary Scranton had bought 'nineteen straw huts and an unsightly strip of unoccupied land' in 1886 as the site for the Ihwa Girls' Primary School, the forerunner of today's renowned Ewha Women's University. The main street through Jong-dong was Legation Street, where, a *Korean Repository* editorial commented in 1896, 'Seoul may well be proud of the substantial brick business blocks. Their concrete foundations are 16 to 20 feet deep, and units have already been taken by a bank, a grocery, and a hardware store. A hotel would be very welcome, also a drug store and a dentists' (Fig. 3.12). Here also was the Seoul Union, whose

3.11 Jong-dong Methodist church, looking north. No 4 marks the Russian legation.

members enjoyed plays and musicals, lectures, and tennis on three courts.

Churches, schools, hospitals, and pharmacies were generally well patronized by Koreans, but of all the Western-style buildings, the one that perhaps meant most to many of the residents of Seoul was more of a monument than a functional building. In 1429 King Sejong had built the Yeongeunmun ('Welcoming Favours Gate'), an honorific archway about half a mile outside the West Gate of Seoul, at which arriving embassies from the Emperor of China were to be welcomed. Extravagant ceremonies and great festivities celebrated this annual occasion. In the late nineteenth century it was still there, but the roadway through the so-called 'Peking Pass' was narrow, and worse, it symbolized subservience to China. When Gojong affirmed Korea's independence before the spirits of the royal ancestors at Jongmyo on 7 January 1895, it was ordered to be demolished, and on 21 November 1896 the foundation stone of a new Independence Arch, modelled on the Arc de Triomphe in Paris, was laid to replace it (Plate 15). A gathering of around five thousand people watched, including foreign diplomats. Boys from Baejae School sang rousing songs and drill was demonstrated by those from the Royal English College. Foreigners applauded the progress of Korea's modernization, but even so the instigator of the new Arch, Seo Jaepil, was under no illusions. In his opinion the situation in Korea was worse than when he had left Seoul for the United States fourteen years before. While accepting the need for reform, he blamed foreign interference for bringing nothing but trouble and suffering. 'The people' he wrote, 'seem to be perfectly helpless, and have no plan whatever as to what they should do to make a living.'

41

3.12 Advertisement in *The Korean Repository*, July 1896. Prices are given in Japanese yen.

4
The Palaces

AFTER THE FRENETIC rush of the modern city, the palaces of
Seoul are havens of calm and a wonderful evocation of
ancient privilege in a world apart. They must also have
seemed so to outsiders in past centuries. Nowadays they are
much less extensive than they were in the Joseon period,
their buildings fewer, the bright five-coloured painting
(*dancheong*) (Plate 19) on much of their woodwork more
faded. Today's visitors may not be conscious of the intense
splendour and drama that once filled these halls and
pathways, yet after they have gone and the sun goes down,
the shadows lengthen, the pigeons coo quietly among the
roof timbers, and the ghosts of past courtiers may still
sometimes be sensed hurrying through the courtyards,
reviving some urgent, long-forgotten business.

Four palaces survive in modern Seoul, walled compounds
containing buildings of stone and wood in Chinese style erected
at various times from the early seventeenth century onwards.
They are known today as Gyeongbok, Changdeok, Deoksu,
and Unhyeon. A fifth, Gyeongdeok ('Celebrating Virtue'), was
built inside the West Gate in 1616 at the cost of several
thousand demolished houses. It was renamed Gyeonghui
('Celebrating Splendour') when King Yeongjo moved into it in
1760 and was referred to as the 'upper palace', but at the end of
the nineteenth century it was commonly known as the
Mulberry Palace after the trees planted in its grounds by a
foreigner in an unsuccessful sericulture project. It was the
setting for the ceremony in 1897 at which King Gojong
inaugurated the Great Han Empire and assumed the title of
Emperor, as 'a vast crowd of white-robed and black-robed men

... looked down upon the striking scene from a hall in the grounds'. It was demolished on Japanese orders in 1910.

The first palace to be built was Gyeongbok ('Shining blessings'), begun in 1394. The architect was Jeong Dojeon, who chose its auspicious name from the Chinese *Book of Odes*. The buildings within its walls epitomized the peak of contemporary architectural skill and tradition and its Audience Hall (*Keunjungchun*) was the setting for the most important state occasions. They were marked by the ringing of a bell in the great Gwanghwa Gate, once the most splendid portico in Korea, its three archways guarded by stone fire-dogs (Fig. 4.1). But a family dispute over the succession caused Taejo's successors to abandon the palace as a royal residence and it gradually fell into disuse. An observatory was built there in 1434, but when the Japanese destroyed much of the city in 1592 the palace was not restored. Only in 1865–7 was it rebuilt on the orders of the Daeweon-gun, at great cost both to the state exchequer and to individual contributors (Plate 16). One of these was the wealthy official Sin Jaehyo,

4.1 Gwanghwa Gate with a guardian fire-dog, outside the Gyeongbok Palace.

an active promoter of *pansori*. Having previously introduced his lover, the singer Jin Chaesu, to the Daeweon-gun in the latter's much smaller Unhyeon Palace, he could then only watch—and compose heartbroken poetry—when she was commanded to perform at the inauguration of the new Palace and was taken by the Daeweongun to be his courtesan.

The history of Gyeongbok (or Western) Palace as a centre of court life came to an end on 8 October 1895 with the assassination of Queen Min (Plate 17). Though an attractive and strong-willed woman, she had played too active a part in the political struggle for her country, and at Japanese instigation a party of discontented Korean soldiers broke into her private quarters. 'They found her, cut her down, and threw her, still breathing, on an oil-soaked pile of brushwood, burning her so completely that only a few charred bones were recovered for burial' (William Sands). Early the next year the King fled in a lady's palanquin with his secondary wife Lady Om to Jong-dong and the refuge of the Russian legation, where he stayed for just over a year. When it was deemed safe for him to leave, on 20 February 1897, it was not back to Gyeongbok or to Changdeok that he went but into the hurriedly reconstructed Deoksu ('Virtuous Long Life') Palace, adjoining the reassuring foreign legation quarter (Plate 18). The narrow streets were lined with soldiers, police, and boys from the Baejae School throwing flowers, so that ordinary people were unable to catch a glimpse of the procession.

Deoksu, previously known as Gyeongun ('Auspicious clouds'), had been the principal royal palace when King Seonjo returned to Seoul in 1593 but it became subsidiary to Changdeok in 1611. There the Lady Om, whom Sands sniffily described as 'raised from kitchenmaid to the first rank of secondary consort', bore Gojong's third son. In the same year, Mrs Bishop wrote that both 'the Eastern and Western Palaces, with their enormous accommodation and immense pleasure-grounds, were deserted, and were already beginning to decay.' Despite the subsequent installation of electric lighting by the Thomas Edison Company, William Sands was also uncomplimentary about Deoksu, describing the new royal residence as a 'crude, hasty structure lacking all dignity and grace ... Its only important feature was the huge granite wall that surrounded and protected it.' Gojong, who began to recover a little of the confidence that he had completely lost in the previous twelve months, evidently valued the security afforded by the wall more highly, as he wandered the lanes around the palace and the legation quarter, talking informally to adults and children.

The palace used by the greatest number of the Joseon kings as their official residence was the eastern, or summer, palace, Changdeok ('Illustrious Virtue') (Plate 19). Built in 1405 as a detached residence (an annex to Gyeongbok) for King Taejong, it was destroyed by the Japanese and rebuilt between 1607 and 1610. Burned down in 1623 and rebuilt by 1647, thirteen kings conducted their government from it until the reoccupation of Gyeongbok in 1868, and today forty-one buildings still stand in its grounds, their brick and plastered walls, decorative tiles, curved eaves, shaped doorways, and carved woodwork all designed to harmonize with the surrounding landscape. Some of the surviving furnishings show signs of the Western influence and taste to which the King and Queen began to succumb in the last decades of the nineteenth century, and in the stables, alongside the royal palanquins, still stands the King's large American car, imported in 1903.

Behind the palace lies the Secret Garden (biweon), a beautiful private park once reserved for the pleasure of the palace women but later opened up for wider court use. Within its walled enclosure the hills and valleys of the undulating countryside were recreated, streams flowing into a lotus pond, walkways and pavilions carefully positioned among groves of trees, bamboo, and flowering shrubs so as to afford ever-changing vistas of colour and wildlife according to the season of the year (Plate 20). Here, by the lotus pond, was built the Yeonghwadang, where in the late eighteenth century tense candidates attended the vital examinations on which their civil service careers depended. Here, in 1776, King Jeongjo began the construction of a new royal library, Gyujanggak. One of its buildings was used for the storage of his own writings and pictures and those of his ancestors, and another for the airing of books, a necessity observed regularly by all scholars to preserve them from humidity and dampness.

Adjacent to Changdeok on its southern side was the Royal Ancestral Shrine (Jongmyo), the most sacred spot in the capital, where the kings of the Joseon dynasty worshipped the tablets of their forebears. In 1592 the Japanese commander Toyotomi Hideyoshi briefly set up his own headquarters there, only to destroy it when he decided to move closer to the South Gate. Rebuilding began in 1608, and the stately and richly colourful ceremony resumed, with musicians and dancers performing the arcane Confucian ritual bestowed upon the Korean king by the emperor of China as far back as 1116. Today's tourists may still see a shortened version of the rite, now dedicated to 27 Joseon kings and their queens (Plates 21 & 22). In 1897, when Gojong assumed the title of Emperor, an Altar of Heaven was built, a small replica of the Chinese Temple of Heaven, and for just thirteen years the Korean monarch offered worship there that put him on a par with the emperors of China and Japan. Such presumption came to an end with the Japanese annexation in 1910, and only a small reminder of the Altar now remains.

First and foremost, the palaces were royal residences, with male and female quarters for the king, the queen, their immediate relatives, the royal children, courtesans, eunuchs, and servants. They contained pavilions which could be put to use for quarantine in times of sickness or for childbirth. But palaces were also the centre of government. In their audience chambers and meeting rooms the king and his closest officials debated national policy and the issuing of edicts. All that went on behind the tall walls of the palaces—whether domestic or political—was so remote from the experience and comprehension of most of Seoul's citizens that they could be forgiven for regarding their royal family with a mixture of awe and fear. Yet the Korean court was far less secretive than its counterpart in Beijing's Forbidden City. There was plenty of coming and going through the palace gates, by royal relatives, officials, soldiers, shamans, entertainers, and servants, and the world outside didn't rest in total ignorance of what was going on inside. Perhaps this was in part due to the fact that the Korean ruler was, until 1897, not imperial but merely royal. Unlike the Chinese Son of Heaven, the Korean king had no semi-divine status. The royal clan was essentially the *primus inter pares* of the yangban class, and might struggle to maintain that position. Autocrat though he might prefer to be, the king was subject to stresses and constraints that were well understood and even exploited by his ministers, rendering his own strength of character critical.

He also had to withstand baleful advice and pressure from the eunuchs, whom Sands called 'probably the most influential people at the Korean court'. Among their duties was supervision of the palace women, of whom there were large numbers, ranging in status from the mother of the king down to the legion of anonymous servant girls. The beautifully dressed courtesans were there to ensure the royal succession by bearing the king's sons. The refined and skilled *gisaeng*, mostly of humble origin and specially trained in music, dance, poetry, and other arts, provided sophisticated entertainment for the court males. There were around seventy of them in Gyeongbok in 1895. Though regarded with disdain by members of the nobility and not permitted to marry, there is little doubt that their lives were passed in much greater comfort than they would have been in the outside world. The shamans had the job of communicating with the spirit world, especially in time of crisis. Behind the scenes, all these women wielded varied and considerable influence. In the late nineteenth century they certainly did not find favour with Queen Min's American physician Lillias Underwood, who described them as 'hardened, coarse and vulgar, ... as depraved as women can be'. All of them, she objected, were smokers. Homer Hulbert, however, who also frequented the palace, took a more lenient view. 'Foreigners often make the mistake of supposing that their position is a disgraceful one, but the palace women are entirely respectable, and any delinquency on their part would be severely dealt with.'

Unnatural though palace life was in its fastidious respect for the rules of Confucian protocol, and paranoid though it was about political scandal, the occupants led cultured and, by the standards of the day, comfortable and enjoyable lives. Yet the palaces were certainly not immune to tragedy. After the Japanese wars nothing significant of either the Changdeok or Gyeongbok palace remained standing, and it was nineteen years before the royal family could again settle down in peace in the rebuilt Changdeok. Fire was a constant hazard, and trauma of an entirely different kind afflicted the court in 1776. The son and heir of King Yeongjo, Crown Prince Sado, suffered from a progressive mental illness which might nowadays be attributed to the unnatural deprivations of his childhood and his perceived rejection by his father. His wife, the faithful Lady Hyegyeong, bore him a son, but as his behaviour became increasingly bizarre the entire court agonized over his patent unsuitability for succession to the throne. Finally, his father ordered him to climb into a cramped rice chest, where he was abandoned and died in agony eight days later, watched by his son, now the new Crown Prince. Nor was this the only torment inflicted on Lady Hyegyeong. In the same year intrigue brought about the execution of her uncle; in 1801 her brother was put to death for professing Catholicism; and the exile of her brother-in-law meant that she was barred from seeing her beloved sister for twenty years. In palace affairs, principle took precedence over relationships and sentiment.

The Chinese court was also subject to physical and political threats, but these didn't compromise the sense of fear in which the dragon throne was generally held by those whose lives were passed on the other side of the great walls. Perhaps the answer to the Korean court's comparative humanity, despite being so different, was a matter of scale: its concealing walls, though high, were not so intimidating as those of the Forbidden City (Fig. 4.2); its compounds, though a haven from the rough world outside, were not as huge and impenetrable as those surrounding the Son of Heaven's terrestrial quarters. Perhaps, on the other hand, the Korean court was better understood because it showed its desire to be so. As in China, the monarch professed acceptance of the Confucian injunction to serve his people. In the Joseon, there were certainly those who put self-interest

4.2 Outside the walls of Gyeongbok Palace (right), looking south towards Namsan.

before the public good: nobody has much of a good word for King Seonjo, whose own subjects shouted insults at the royal procession as it fled from the Japanese in 1592. But the greatest of all Korean kings showed that they wanted to live up to their responsibilities. The eighteenth-century monarchs Yeongjo and his grandson Jeongjo both took seriously their Confucian duty to understand their people's needs. In his long fifty-two year reign, Yeongjo met commoners at the palace gate at least once a year, as well as visiting the markets to listen to merchants' concerns. Jeongjo went further and extended the system for submitting petitions, permitting plaintiffs to stop him on his frequent extramural processions to the tombs of his ancestors and learning about such grievances as official corruption,

51

excessive taxation, and unfair business competition. Concerned for the welfare of the poorest people, he abolished the government office that hunted down runaway slaves, endeavoured to protect abandoned children, forbade the illegal use of torture and execution, and distributed sacks of grain to poor households. The upper classes probably appreciated more his formal gestures of recognition, such as his periodic orders for the honouring of sixty-, seventy-, and eighty-year olds with parties and the distribution of gifts. In 1794 he gave a grand party for his mother Lady Hyegyeong's sixtieth birthday. Fifteen years later, his son King Sunjo gave another to celebrate the sixtieth anniversary of the consummation of her marriage (Plate 23).

No Chinese emperor had ever been so diligent about listening to ordinary people. Nevertheless, in the formality and ceremonial of its routine much Korean court life was based on Chinese patterns. Its ritual seemed appropriate to the Chinese ambassador Dong Yue in 1487 ('Though we could not understand the music we could catch the thought of the ceremony, it being modelled after that of China'), but it would have been as strange to ordinary Koreans then as it is today to the tourists who witness an abbreviated version of it at the annual Jongmyo ritual. The Confucian liturgy and its associated music and dance were slow and precisely controlled, and dated from a different age and different environment. Details of performances were meticulously preserved in print and pictorial form between the late eighteenth and early twentieth centuries in the series of books and paintings known as *uigwe*, which provide a glimpse into the colourful and strangely disciplined way of life within the palaces (Plate 24).

5

The Foreign Community

THE FOREIGN COMMUNITY in late nineteenth-century Seoul was not large. The Chinese were the most numerous: it was easy for them to come and go, and many of them were shopkeepers in Seoul. They fled during the Sino–Japanese War of 1894–5 but soon returned to reopen their premises. The Japanese colony, rising from 1,438 in 1895 to 2,366 in 1901, was concentrated near the South Gate. There, wrote Sands, the Japanese minister 'lived in his citadel as in a feudal castle', surrounded by his police courts, schools, newspaper offices, and priests, and protected by 'a miniature army, with artillery, cavalry and infantry, engineers and field telegraph corps'. Most Westerners lived near their legations in Jong-dong. The July 1896 *Korean Repository* refers to '150 European and American residents in Seoul, and large numbers of Western soldiers and marines spending there [sic] pay here'. According to Mrs Bishop, there were 65 British subjects in Korea in January 1897, of whom the majority presumably lived in Seoul. These relatively few Westerners played a prominent part in the story of Seoul's growth.

To counter Japan's growing influence after the Treaty of Ganghwa, the Chinese statesman Li Hongzhang dispatched Yuan Shikai and Ma Jianzhong as envoys and a Prussian, Paul-Georg von Möllendorff, to set up a Korean branch of the Chinese Maritime Customs Service. Von Möllendorff arrived in Seoul on 13 December 1882, 'stared at by a crowd of thousands', and had his first audience with King Gojong on Boxing Day. During his three years in Seoul he exercised great power, holding such titles as Vice-Minister of Foreign Affairs and Defence and Director of the National Mint, and he successfully laid the foundations of a Customs service which brought invaluable revenue to the Korean government. He helped Korea to establish diplomatic relations with Britain, Germany, Italy, Russia, and Belgium, though European recognition was not automatically translated into acknowledgement of Korean independence. Great Britain, for example, accepted the Chinese claim to dominion over the peninsular kingdom, nominating its envoy to Beijing as concurrent plenipotentiary to Seoul and appointing a consul-general in the Korean capital (Fig. 5.1).

The first American minister sent to Seoul under the terms of the 1882 Treaty was Lucius Foote, who arrived in May 1883 to a warm welcome from King Gojong. The Queen's nephew, Min Yeong-ik, departed for the United States with a request for specialists to come and advise the Korean court on modernization, and George Foulk was posted from Yokohama as naval attaché, arriving on 5 June 1884. His interests extended far beyond the navy, and he helped plant

5.1 The British Consulate-General in 1888.

American vegetable seed at the government farm and gave advice on gold-mining methods, breeding cattle, and even furniture design. It was, however, more than four years before Washington sent the military experts that Gojong principally sought.

Foulk and von Möllendorff saw each other as rivals for Gojong's favours and disliked each other, and Foulk was instrumental in the Prussian's recall to China on suspicion of unduly favouring Russian interests. But Li Hongzhang himself criticized von Möllendorff for encouraging too much Korean independence, and sent two Americans from China, Henry Merrill as Chief Customs Commissioner and Judge Owen Denny as adviser to the Home and Foreign Offices, with instructions to restore Chinese authority. He also nominated Yuan Shikai as Chinese Resident Minister and Commissioner for Trade. Yuan was still only twenty-nine, but his overbearing manner already revealed the personal ambition that would eventually lead him to claim the imperial throne in China, and the Westerners in Seoul generally disliked him. For his part, he resented Gojong's efforts to use the United States to balance competing Japanese and Chinese interests. He disapproved of Foulk's agricultural work and purchase of US-built steamers, and had him recalled in 1887. He resented Horace Allen's hospital, and took some of its first nurses as his concubines. Critics saw him as possibly the most powerful man in Seoul.

There was no automatic sense of bonding among the foreigners, even among those of shared nationality and common purpose. Although friendships were formed between individuals of different nationality, rivalry and suspicion were never far below the surface. Foulk regarded his minister Foote as a coward for fleeing the country in the aftermath of the December 1884 rioting, and though a

Christian himself, was critical of what he described as 'ignoramuses' among the missionary community whose 'miserable petty jealousy is very great'. Of Gojong's foreign advisers, the American William Sands took up his appointment in 1900 at the age of twenty-five, two years after arriving in the US legation. Four years later he admitted disappointment that, despite what he called his 'reformist spirit', he had been unable to 'unite the various foreign advisers ... into one body serving the interests of the country that supported them. They necessarily still thought of themselves as agents of their own legations'.

Gojong and Queen Min had been friendly to the foreign community from the very beginning, taking advice from the men, giving audiences to their wives, consulting their physicians, supporting their missions, and entertaining them at skating parties on the Palace lake. Discomfited as the visitors sometimes were to find that court business was conducted at night, after the imposition of the curfew, they were also flattered to be given direct access to the King and Queen in the private rooms of the Gyeongbok Palace and even permission to photograph them. Mrs Bishop took a picture for Queen Victoria and Gojong seemed not to mind that Western diplomats bullied him by insisting on seeing him whenever they wished to discuss something. Privately, however, he might have felt less charitable towards Lord Curzon, who before visiting Korea in 1892 had called it 'one of the dirtiest and most repulsive countries in the world', and when his arrival in Seoul was delayed by a shortage of ponies, 'got very angry, explained that he was one of the most important people in England, and that it was a matter of most vital importance that he should see the King that week; and he threatened beatings and dismissals all round' (C. Spring Rice).

One of the most influential and successful foreigners in Seoul was the Irishman John McLeavey Brown. His Korean career began in 1893 when he was sent from China to join the Customs Service. In 1896 he became Chief Financial Adviser to the government, and two years later was promoted to be Chief Commissioner for Customs and Controller of Finances. As such, he was responsible for an income of some US$500,000 from the treaty ports, around ten per cent of all government revenue. He was also charged with limiting royal expenditure, and the size of his problem may be gauged from the fact that to pay bills associated with Gojong's fiftieth birthday celebrations on 7 September 1901, the government borrowed US$500,000 from the First National Bank. He is particularly credited with cleaning up the streets of Seoul and designing the modern environs of Pagoda Park. He was a strong-willed character, and the equally determined Isabella Bird Bishop, the first woman to become a member of the Royal Geographical Society, stayed with him during her fourth visit to Korea in 1897. What forthright conversations they must have had!

Not all foreigners cut such impressive figures. Foote's successor as US minister, William Parker, was incapacitated by drink and was replaced by Foulk on 1 September 1886, though Washington did not see fit either to raise the salary of the former naval attaché or even to replace his furniture, which had been destroyed in the looting the previous year. Two military advisers, Edmund H. Cummins and John G. Lee, went the same way as Parker and were dismissed for dereliction of duty in September 1889, leaving their compatriots William Dye and J. H. Nienstead to train 155 non-commissioned officers and 12,000 soldiers. Discipline in the recently established Military Academy (*Yeonmu Gongweon*) was poor, and despite their noble efforts it was plainly an impossible task. The outbreak of the Donghak rebellion on 26 April 1894, the same day as the new US Minister John Sill arrived in Seoul, brought rival Chinese and Japanese armies to the peninsula and the brink of the Sino–Japanese War. The Japanese had Dye dismissed.

Most of the Westerners in Seoul represented mission boards, principally the American Presbyterian and American Methodist Episcopalian Missions. They had first arrived to find an official ban on proselytizing, and the going was not easy. Like other expatriates, the missionaries were generally in their twenties and were inevitably prey to lapses of temperament despite their vocation. Some had previous Asian experience, others did not. Deprived of home comforts and prompt support, they were prone to sectarian rivalry and personal antipathies as well as physical sickness. Following the illegal acquisition of land by the Roman Catholics in 1888 for a new cathedral, the interdict against Christianity was reiterated in Seoul. As many Protestant missionaries continued to teach, preach, and sing hymns publicly, rumours spread of the ill-treatment and even eating of babies, prompting an ugly anti-Christian mood which the government stepped in to quell. Suspicion nevertheless persisted about converts' motives, with hostility coming particularly from Confucian traditionalists: 'One of the Christians here who this spring refused to sacrifice at his father's tomb showed me a scar on his forehead which he received from his aunt, who knocked him senseless with an inkstone' (Samuel Moffett). Even so, the churches' fortunes continued to rise, and by 1905 the number of native Protestants—just 150 in 1890—had grown to some 15,000.

Outstanding among the first missionaries was Horace Allen, who became one of Korea's staunchest friends and advocates. Having arrived in Seoul on 22 September 1884 as a medical missionary for the American Presbyterian Church, he was almost immediately instrumental in saving the life of Min Yeong-ik when he was wounded in the December coup attempt. This persuaded King Gojong to give approval for Allen's mission hospital, which opened on 9 April 1885 with twenty outpatients. The following year he authorized an affiliated medical and scientific school, and gave permission for it to move into the former home of Hong Yeongsik, killed during the disturbances. Here the Jejungweon ('House of Civilised Virtue'), as it was called, had forty beds, a dispensary, and an operating theatre. Patients who could afford it were charged US$1,000 per day for a single room, or $399 a day in a ward. In contrast the Methodist William Scranton worked among the poorest and neediest members of Seoul society, those forced by contagious diseases to leave their homes and live in tents. He opened a hospital on 15 June 1886, the year in which Annie Ellers also opened a women's department in the government hospital.

The great missionary teacher Homer Hulbert described the Korean character as 'highly conservative' but responsive to innovation when self-interest was involved. He cited the fact that until the 1870s they had known only flint and steel as means of lighting fire, but that when friction matches were introduced as a consequence of the foreign treaties, they took to them easily. More significant, perhaps, was the fact that foreign example prompted the government to open new schools, using both Chinese characters and *hangeul* (Fig. 5.2) and teaching arithmetic, history, and geography. The Royal College, later the Royal English School, was founded in 1886 as the first government training establishment for future administrators. When it failed to gain recognition from the yangban it was reformed by the king in 1894 under

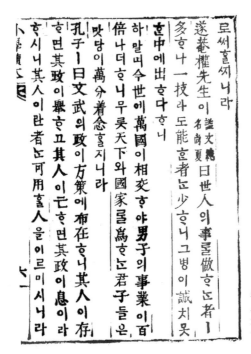

5.2 A page from *Sohak Dogbon*, a school book in Chinese and *hangeul* typography.

the Englishman William Hutchinson, who particularly impressed William Sands by playing soccer with his Korean boys, cooking dinner for them, and then making music 'far into the early morning'.

In addition to the Royal English School, language schools were set up to teach French, Japanese, and Russian. There was also a law school and one devoted to teacher training. But enrolments were slow to rise, nine schools in 1901 registering no more than 630 pupils. The mission schools, where the curriculum included history, general science, and patriotism, were equally slow to overcome yangban prejudice. In 1897 their pupils numbered around eight hundred. Pre-eminent among them was the American

Methodist Episcopal Church's Baejae hakdang, founded in 1885 by the Rev. Henry Appenzeller, who later edited *The Korean Repository*. It was awarded its name, 'Nourishing Talent Academy', by King Gojong. Here the ethos was similar to that of the English public school, combining both compulsory chapel attendance and military drill, but the syllabus was more that of a liberal arts college than of the progressive, practical academy that Korea needed. On 2 September 1896 its students all marched to the Russian Embassy and cheered the King, 'an innovation, we hear, that was pleasant to their sovereign' (*The Korean Repository*).

The task of establishing schools for girls was begun by the Rev. William Scranton's mother, Mary, whose institution opened its doors in November 1886 and so pleased Queen Min that she coined its name, 'Pear-blossom School' (*Ihwa hakdang*). Mrs Scranton tried to visit homes to encourage parents to send girls to school, but 'Our presence on the streets in too close proximity to the women's apartments was oftentimes the signal for the rapid closing of doors and speedy retreat behind screens, while children ran screaming.' After two years Ihwa had eighteen pupils, and no more than fifty after ten years.

In deciding what and how to teach, always bearing in mind their prime obligation of spreading the gospel, missionary teachers had to tread carefully, especially those who sought to educate girls. As Miss L. C. Rothweiler wrote in her article 'What shall we teach in our girls' schools?' in *The Korean Repository* (March 1892), 'We hope, though it may be years before this hope is realized, to have other girls than only those who are exposed to all the vices of the streets'. She emphasized teaching mainly practical subjects such as making and mending clothes and food preparation. The medium of instruction was *hangeul*, with limited teaching of English and Chinese. According to Lillias Underwood, 'it is a great mistake to unfit these girls by a foreign education for the homes they are to fill, and we only seek to make Christian Koreans of them, not American ladies.'

Horace Allen was sucked, not unwillingly, into political activity, and growing disillusioned with some of his colleagues' heavy-handed approach to evangelization, and having spent two years back in Washington assisting the first Korean embassy there, he accepted full-time appointment as Secretary to the American Legation in Seoul in 1890. On 23 July 1894 Japanese troops entered the Gyeongbok Palace, imprisoning the King. Wives of foreign diplomats, including Mrs Allen and the wife of the Russian minister, Mrs Waeber, sustained him, but he refused anything but boiled eggs and milk. When a new pro-Japanese cabinet ushered in the Gabo reforms Seoul began to suffer shortages (see Chapter 2). William Dye had remained to train the palace guard, but it proved ineffective on 8 October 1895 when Japanese soldiers again assisted the assault on the palace in which Queen Min was assassinated. Dye, however, together with Allen and Horace Underwood, managed to save Gojong and organize his flight to the Russian Embassy. There the influence of the US Minister, as Allen now was, on his friend Gojong continued to be profound. He helped to select a fresh, anti-Japanese cabinet; he won franchises for American companies to develop the first railway and the rich Unsan gold mine; and he cooperated with John McLeavey Brown and Seo Jaepil in trying to reform the economic and political systems of Korea. But as Japanese power increased his influence declined, and in 1905 he returned to the United States.

Russia, whose soldiers had been in Seoul since 1890 at the King's request, provided military advisers to succeed the Americans in the Military Academy (Fig. 5.3). However,

5.3 Korean soldiers with Russian instructors, a photo taken by Isabella Bishop in 1895.

protests at the growth of Russian influence now prompted the King to dispense with them. Moreover, when thirty Americans and Europeans recruited in Shanghai arrived in Seoul on 14 September 1898 to serve in the palace bodyguard, the Independence Club objected and they were sent back to China in less than a fortnight. The King was at least showing an awareness of public opinion. By now, however, events were moving rapidly towards the dénouement with which the new century began. When Japan defeated Russia and established its **Protectorate** over Korea in 1905, members of the foreign community in Seoul may have been taken by surprise, but the long-held fears of many Koreans were realized.

Historians argue over the causes of the enormous changes Korea underwent in the late Joseon era and throughout the twentieth century, and whether they were primarily native or foreign. Whether or not Koreans could themselves have begun the hard process of reform and modernization, it is certain that foreigners played a critical part in the momentous events of the last two decades of the nineteenth century. They also left plentiful first-hand accounts of them. Often these are neither objective nor dispassionate, nor are they unanimous in their judgements. Like the accounts of many other parts of the world discovered by late Victorians with political, mercantile, and missionary objectives, they betray the prejudices of their own age. They are nonetheless invaluable evidence of a disappearing and tumultuous age, and in many cases they mask a sincere liking for Korea along with genuine attempts to understand and help its people. The strength of the modern Korean–Western alliance is due in no small part to them.

Glossary

Daeweon-gun, the
Father of King Gojong. An ambitious man, he was the effective ruler during the nominal regency of the Dowager Queen Sinjeong from 1864 to 1873, and thereafter continued to play an active political role. By rebuilding the Gyeongbok Palace he planned to restore the glories of the early Joseon dynasty. Though his wife was a Catholic, he ordered the execution of Catholics in Seoul in 1866, partly because they advocated a Korean treaty with Britain and France to counter a perceived Russian threat. Britain and France had themselves only recently destroyed the Summer Palace in Beijing and exacted humiliating treaty rights.

Dancheong
The traditional craft of decorating important governmental and religious buildings in five colours (red, blue/green, yellow, black, and white). Categories included floral, animal, and geometric patterns, and scenes from the life of Buddha.

Donghak rebellion
A major peasant rebellion (1894–5) proclaiming social egalitarianism, protesting against corrupt administration, and seeking land reform. Based on the quasi-nationalistic, quasi-religious teachings of Choe Je-u (1824–64), it drew particular support in the south-west at a time when many Koreans in traditional trades were losing out to foreign commercial competition and Christian teachings appeared to threaten traditional society.

Gabo reforms
Name popularly given to the reform measures, some two thousand in total, framed by a new Advisory Council headed by Gim Hongjip and approved by King Gojong between July 1894 and February 1896. They are so called after the name of the year, *Gabo*, in which they were first introduced. They included revisions to central government organization, local government, the monetary and examination systems, military and judicial structures and procedures, and outdated aspects of the social system.

Gisaeng
A professional class of girls and women highly trained in the arts of poetry, music, dance, and other forms of social entertainment. They were not to be hired in the manner of prostitutes, but sexual services for important patrons provided them with opportunities for political influence and they might become secondary wives. Their social status was nevertheless low.

65

Gwangdae

Itinerant popular entertainers. They generally represented distinctive regional cultures, though some of their acts and songs transcended mountain and riverine barriers. Like all entertainers they were low class, but they were not excluded from the palaces and were one of the court's sources of public opinion.

Hangeul

The Korean alphabet of 28 symbols, largely invented by King Sejong and published in late 1443 or early 1444. Sejong saw the value of being able to keep records in the vernacular language, but the literati called it *eun mun* ('vulgar script') and for more than three centuries continued to use Chinese characters exclusively.

Independence Club

Founded in July 1896 by young Koreans advocating democratization, modernization, and self-strengthening in education and industry, but also seeking to eradicate imperialistic foreign influence. It held weekly debates and published the *Dongnip Sinmun* ('Independent') newspaper. It advocated use of the Korean national flag and national anthem, and supported Gojong's adoption of the title Emperor in 1897. Japanese pressure led to its suppression in November 1897, when members were given long prison sentences.

Nectar paintings (*gamnojeong*)

A type of temple painting practised in the eighteenth and nineteenth centuries depicting Buddhist deities, services for the dead ('nectar rites'), and scenes of daily life on earth and in hell. They are valuable as sources of information on popular beliefs and practices.

Pansori

A form of dramatic storytelling by a single singer with a drum accompanist. It employs a mixture of sung narrative and spoken passages which include repartee between the two performers. It may have originated in the eighteenth century, but enjoyed its greatest popularity in the nineteenth century, when even members of the yangban class sponsored it, even though the stories were full of social satire attacking the corruption of the local gentry and Buddhist clergy.

Peungsu ('Wind and water')

The ancient Chinese practice of geomancy (*fengshui*), the interpretation of natural phenomena used to determine auspicious locations and dates, e.g. for siting buildings and tombs, and holding weddings and funerals.

Protectorate
On 17 November 1905, after King Gojong had been confined within his palace by soldiers for two days, the Japanese compelled the Korean Foreign Minister to sign a Protectorate Treaty. With the professed aim of affording Korea peaceful modernization, this gave Japan authority over aspects of Korean foreign and diplomatic policy, with effectively unlimited control over the Korean government and people. Ito Hirobumi was nominated as its first Resident-General in Seoul, and on 22 June 1907 Gojong was forced to abdicate. The five-year period leading to complete colonial annexation in 1910 was marked by severe repression of Korean freedom.

Shaman (*mudang*)
A practitioner of the 'religion' based on contacting the spirit world while in a state of trance. Korean shamanism was inherited from Siberia and had an ancient history. By the Joseon dynasty most shamans were female, and handed their occupation down from mother to daughter. They were used by all classes of society, including members of the court, and through their arcane rites many exercised considerable power in local communities. Queen Min favoured one called Jilyeong-gun in the 1890s.

Slaves
Hereditary members, through the mother's line, of the lowest class of Korean society, belonging either to the government or private households. They were sometimes given by kings as a form of reward for military or political prowess, and could be bought and sold. Male occupations ranged from farm labourer to craft worker, female occupations from washerwoman to prostitute. Frequently ill-treated in earlier periods, they were becoming less easily distinguishable from free members of the sangmin class through the nineteenth century.

Uigwe ('Rubrics')
Rules for the conduct of court ceremonies, banquets, and entertainments held between 1719 and 1902.

Yangban ('Two classes')
Members of the ruling social élite. The name refers to the two orders of civil and military officers on whom kings relied in the Goryeo dynasty (918–1392), but later came to apply to the gentry as a whole. Membership of the class was determined by education rather than wealth, and official posts were open only to members of yangban clans. Before the Hideyoshi wars, only clans with recognized yangban lineages were acknowledged, but subsequently those whose success in trade or industry had allowed them

to buy the necessary education began to infiltrate the class. At the same time, some of those from clans which had traditionally relied on official appointments now turned instead to estate management. There was a clear hierarchy within the yangban class: post-holders were ranked into nine major and many subsidiary grades, and members of central administration were superior to those holding provincial posts. Genuine academics who devoted themselves to bookwork and the defence of public morals were sometimes known as 'mountain' or 'country scholars'.

Selected Bibliography

Books by Westerners who lived in late Joseon Seoul:

Allen, Horace, *Things Korean: a Collection of Sketches and Anecdotes Missionary and Diplomatic*, New York 1908, repr. Seoul 1975.

Bird Bishop, Isabella, *Korea and her Neighbours*, London 1897, repr. KPI 1985.

Carles, W.R., *Life in Corea*, London 1888.

Gale, James Scarth, *Korean Sketches*, New York 1898, repr. Seoul 1973.

Hulbert, Homer, *The Passing of Korea*, Seoul 1906, repr. Yonsei University Press 1969.

Lowell, Percival, *Choson, the Land of the Morning Calm*, Boston: Tickner & Co. 1885.

Miln, Louise, *Quaint Korea*, London 1895.

Sands, William, *Undiplomatic Memories: the Far East 1896–1904*, New York 1930, repr. Seoul 1975, and as *At the Court of Korea, Undiplomatic Memories*, London: Century Hutchinson 1987.

Underwood, Lillias, *Fifteen Years among the Topknots*, New York 1904, repr. Seoul 1977.

Underwood, Lillias, *Underwood of Korea*, New York 1918, repr. Seoul 1983 (a life of Horace G. Underwood by his widow).

Periodicals published by Westerners in late Joseon Korea:

The Korea Review, ed. Homer Hulbert, Seoul 1901–5, monthly.

The Korean Repository, Seoul 1892–8, monthly; repr. Seoul 1975, 5 vols.

Modern sources:

Bennett, Terry, *Korea: Caught in Time*, Reading: Garnet Publishing 1997 (a history of photography in Korea, illustrated with many examples from the late Joseon period).

Cho Pung-you, *Contemporary Views of Yi Dynasty Korea* (in Korean), 2 vols., Seoul 1986 (originally published in Tokyo by Kokusho Kanko-kai as *Mede Miru Richo-jidai*; a substantial collection of early photographs of Korea, mostly taken before and around 1910).

Clark, Donald, and Grayson, J.H., *Discovering Seoul*, Seoul 1986.

Harrington, F.H., *God, Mammon and the Japanese. Dr Horace N. Allen and Korean-American Relations, 1884–1905*, University of Wisconsin Press 1966.

Henderson, Gregory, 'A History of the Chong Dong area and the American embassy residence compound', *Transactions of the Korea Branch, Royal Asiatic Society*, vol. 30, Seoul 1959.

Hur Young-hwan, 'Choson Dynasty Maps of Seoul', *Korea Journal*, vol.30 no.6, June 1990.

Kwon Oh-chang, *Korean Costumes during the Chosun Dynasty*, Seoul 1998.

Lee, K.B., trans. Wagner, E., *A New History of Korea*, Harvard University Press 1984.

Lee, Peter H., ed., *Sourcebook of Korean Civilization*, Columbia University Press, vol. 1 1993, vol. 2 1996.

Nahm, Andrew, *Korea, Tradition and Transformation*, Seoul 1988.

Paik, L. George, *The History of Protestant Missions in Korea 1832–1910*, Pyongyang 1927, 3rd ed. (rev.) Seoul 1980.

Pratt, K.L. and Rutt, R., *Korea, a Historical and Cultural Dictionary*, Richmond: Curzon Press 1999.

Underwood, Peter, Samuel Moffett, Norman Sibley, eds., *First Encounters, Korea 1888–1910*, Seoul 1982 (photographs of late Joseon Korea, with special emphasis on missionary work).

Wagner, Edward, 'Social Stratification in Seventeenth-Century Korea: some pages from a 1663 Seoul Census Register', *Occasional Papers on Korea*, 1, Seattle 1974.

Index